D0050109

100
AFRICAN-AMERICANS
WHO SHAPED AMERICAN HISTORY

Chrisanne Beckner

A Bluewood Book

Published in 2020 by
Bluewood Books
A Division of The Siyeh Group, Inc.,
P.O. Box 23
San Mateo, CA 94401

ISBN 0-912517-18-2

Printed in the USA

Edited and designed by
Ruth DeJauregui

Cover illustration by
Vadim Vahrameev

Illustrated by Tony Chikes

About the author:
Chrisanne Beckner is a writer living in San Francisco, California. She has also written *100 Great Cities of World History* and edited several other books.

TABLE OF CONTENTS

1.   2.   3.   4.   5.
6.   7.

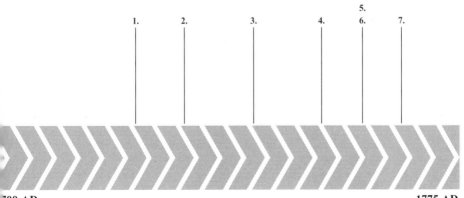

1700 AD

1775 AD

26. GRANVILLE T. WOODS   *33*
1856-1910
27. IDA B. WELLS-BARNETT   *34*
1862-1931
28. MARY CHURCH. TERRELL   *35*
1863-1954
29. GEORGE WASHINGTON CARVER   *36*
c. 1864-1943
30. MATTHEW HENSON   *37*
1866-1955
31. MADAME C.J. WALKER   *38*
1867-1919
32. W.E.B. DU BOIS   *39*
1868-1963
33. JOHN HOPE   *40*
1868-1936
34. SCOTT JOPLIN   *41*
1868-1917
35. ROBERT ABBOTT   *42*
1870-1940
36. JAMES WELDON JOHNSON   *43*
1871-1938
37. PAUL LAURENCE DUNBAR   *44*
1872-1906
38. WILLIAM M. TROTTER   *45*
1872-1934

39. WILLIAM CHRISTOPHER HANDY   *4*
1873-1958
40. ARTHUR SCHOMBURG   *47*
1874-1938
41. MARY McLEOD BETHUNE   *48*
1875-1955
42. GARRETT A. MORGAN   *49*
1875-1963
43. CARTER G. WOODSON   *50*
1875-1950
44. JACK JOHNSON   *51*
1878-1946
45. OSCAR MICHEAUX   *52*
1884-1951
46. MARCUS GARVEY   *53*
1887-1940
47. CLAUDE McKAY   *54*
1889-1948
48. A. PHILIP RANDOLPH   *55*
1889-1979
49. MORDECAI W. JOHNSON   *56*
1890-1976
50. BESSIE COLEMAN   *57*
1892-1926
51. FREDERICK McKINLEY JONES   *58*
1893-1961

8.
9.   11.   10.   12. 13.   14.   15.   16. 17.   18.   19.   2(
                                                                                            2►

1775 AD   **1850 A**

52. WALTER F. WHITE *59*
1893-1955
53. E. FRANKLIN FRAZIER *60*
1894-1962
54. BESSIE SMITH *61*
1894-1937
55. CHARLES H. HOUSTON *62*
1895-1950
56. BENJAMIN E. MAYS *63*
1895-1984
57. PAUL ROBESON *64*
1898-1976
58. DUKE ELLINGTON *65*
1899-1974
59. PERCY LAVON JULIAN *66*
1899-1975
60. LOUIS ARMSTRONG *67*
1900-1971
61. ZORA NEALE HURSTON *68*
1901-1960
62. ROY WILKINS *69*
1901-1981
63. MARIAN ANDERSON *70*
1902-1993

64. LANGSTON HUGHES *71*
1902-1967
65. RALPH BUNCHE *72*
1904-1971
66. DR. CHARLES R. DREW *73*
1904-1950
67. THURGOOD MARSHALL *74*
1908-1993
68. ADAM CLAYTON POWELL, JR. *75*
1908-1972
69. RICHARD WRIGHT *76*
1908-1960
70. KATHERINE DUNHAM *77*
1909-2006
71. BAYARD RUSTIN *78*
1910-1987
72. ROSA PARKS *79*
1913-2005
73. JESSE OWENS *80*
1913-1980
74. KENNETH B. CLARK *81*
1914-2005
74. BILLIE HOLIDAY *82*
1915-1959

850 AD

1925 AD

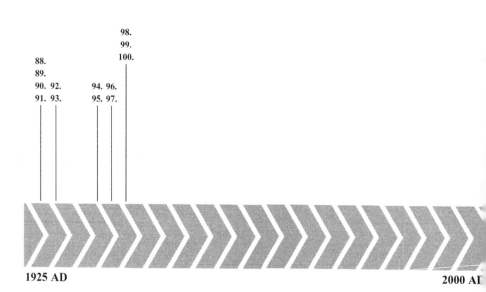

98.
99.
88.   100.
89.
90. 92.   94. 96.
91. 93.   95. 97.

1925 AD   2000 AD

INTRODUCTION

American history is full of the deeds of heroes and heroines: the great educators, the great entertainers, the great thinkers and inventors, the great athletes. What's exciting is that some of the most fascinating events of history are also events of African-American history, and some of the most inspiring heroes of American history are African-American heroes.

African-American history follows the success of a people under challenging circumstances. Through the unity of black churches, the black press, and educational institutions like **Tuskegee Institute, Howard University** and **Spelman College**, African-Americans taught one another how to excel. **Mary McLeod Bethune** started with a one room schoolhouse built on a dumping ground. This one room has grown into the **Bethune-Cookman College**. **Thurgood Marshall** started as a student of lawyer **Charles Houston**, and went on to win a Supreme Court case against segregation in schools. He was later elected to the Supreme Court himself.

Men and women as glamorous as **Harry Belafonte** and **Ruby Dee, Paul Robeson** and **Bill Cosby** did more than entertain us with their voices, their Broadway talent, and their movies. They brought us honest representations of African-Americans that destroyed preconceived stereotypes. **Langston Hughes, Maya Angelou, Lorraine Hansberry, Richard Wright** and **James Baldwin** told the stories that developed into a nationally recognized canon.

W.E.B. Du Bois published *Crisis* magazine. **T. Thomas Fortune** advocated militant resistance to racism. **Booker T. Washington** and **Ida B. Wells-Barnett** used oration and journalism to educate communities on violence and also on opportunity.

Great scientists and inventors have flourished. **George Washington Carver** created peanut butter. Dr. **Charles Drew** discovered that preservable blood plasma could save the lives of thousands because it could be used in transfusions for all blood types. Dr. **Daniel Hale Williams** performed the first heart surgery.

One of the athletic heroes who have made the US world famous is **Jesse Owens**, who won four gold medals at the 1936 Olympics in Berlin, Germany. **Muhammad Ali** became the world champion in boxing. **Wilma Rudolph** overcame polio to win three gold medals in the 1960 Olympics.

Courage led women like **Harriet Tubman** to risk their lives leading people north to freedom, and it led women like **Fannie Lou Hamer** to risk their lives in the struggle for voting rights.

Men like **Malcolm X** and Dr. **Martin Luther King, Jr.** lost their lives in pursuit of civil rights and equality in America. They are two of our most valuable role models in the current struggle for an improved society. All one hundred of these men and women keep the spirit fed with hope.

CRISPUS ATTUCKS
1723-1770

Crispus Attucks, one of the first patriots to give his life in the struggle for American independence, was born in Massachusetts in 1723. With African and Natick Indian ancestors, Attucks' only chance for freedom was to escape from slave owner **William Brown**. At the age of 27, Attucks ran away from Brown's home and joined the crew of a boat sailing away from Boston Harbor. For the next 20 years, Attucks was a man of the sea.

As a sailor on cargo ships and whalers, Attucks developed an independence that not only made him a brave leader among sailors, but a leader of patriot revolutionaries as well. On the night of March 5, 1770, at the age of 47, Attucks' dedication to liberty made American history.

Tension between the Boston patriots and the British soldiers was boiling that spring. British forces were installed to impose order — a fragile order at best — and the ubiquitous threat of violence kept colonists in a high state of agitation. **Hugh Montgomery**, one of the British soldiers, was guarding the Customs House when a young boy came up and insulted him. Montgomery struck out and injured the boy, whose cries rang through the streets, calling people from their homes. Crispus Attucks came forward. He decided immediately, living in a society already on the verge of revolt, that this act of violence would not be tolerated.

Within minutes, a crowd had gathered behind Attucks, who was heading straight for the Customs House. He approached Montgomery personally, insults were exchanged, and soon the crowd took up chunks of ice and snowballs that they threw at the British soldier.

Twelve others appeared, armed and ready, but Attucks, wielding a heavy stick, yelled, "Don't be afraid. Knock 'em over. They dare not fire." It was the first cry of the coming revolution.

The soldiers responded in panic, firing wildly into the crowd, killing Attucks and his supporter **Samuel Gray** immediately. Nine other men were shot in the ensuing battle. Three of them died.

The crowd was soon subdued, but news of the massacre was electric, igniting out rage and shock, along with a new sense of purpose. Thousands came to Attucks funeral, and seven British soldiers were brought to trial for murder, though each was exonerated.

This first revolt would come to be known as the **Boston Massacre**, one of the first battles to mark the beginning of the **American Revolution**. **John Adams** later said "On that night, the foundations of American independence were laid."

It was Crispus Attucks who cared enough about personal freedom to risk his life for its reward, even if that reward would only be available to those who came after.

Crispus Attucks.

BENJAMIN BANNEKER
1731-1806

Benjamin Banneker was one of Ameri-
a's first and finest scientists, as well as one
of Thomas Jefferson's great influences. He
as born in 1731 to the daughter of Molly
Walsh, a former indentured servant in her
native England. Both mother and daughter
purchased slaves in Maryland who later
became their husbands.

Benjamin loved learning to read and
write from Molly's family Bible, but once he
began attending a Quaker school, he knew
his great love was mathematics. He studied
so passionately that he would create his own
problems just for the joy of solving them.

His early interest made him a wise
inventor when he decided to recreate a
pocket watch he saw on a traveling salesman. Since no watches existed in America,
Benjamin Banneker used all his mathemat-
ical skill to develop plans, make the right
calculations, and personally carve each gear
of the first American watch. Made entirely
of wood, Banneker's watch ran perfectly
for over 40 years.

Banneker's passion for exactness also
extended to the study of astronomy. In 1789,
he predicted a solar eclipse that, to the surprise of skeptical astronomers, occurred just
as he'd said it would on April 14.

His brilliance extended also into the
realm of human rights. After reading
Thomas Jefferson's doctrine that "all men
are created equal; that they are endowed by
their Creator with certain unalienable
rights, and that among these are life, liberty,
and the pursuit of happiness," and knowing
that Jefferson owned slaves, Banneker was
moved to write back. In an extremely eloquent letter, Banneker told Jefferson that
African-Americans were equal to white
Americans in intelligence, and therefore
equally entitled to rights and privileges. As
proof, he included a copy of his almanac, a
yearly publication documenting holidays,
coming eclipses, and the hours of sunrise

Benjamin Banneker.

and sunset. Banneker's almanac included
essays on the abolition of slavery as well.

Jefferson wrote back with a new egalitarian stand on the issue of race. A respectful friendship formed, and remained strong
even after Jefferson became the president of
the United States.

Banneker went on to become one of the
foremost astronomers of his age, as well as
one of the men chosen to lay out the new
capital city of Washington D.C. in 1791.
After **Pierre Charles L'Enfant**, the French
city planner, quit and took all his plans back
to France, it was Banneker who reproduced
them from memory.

In October, 1806, after a lifetime of sci-
entific discovery, Benjamin Banneker died,
leaving Americans a more accurate vision
of "freedom for all."

Elizabeth Freeman, one of the most successful abolitionists of the 18th century, was raised in Massachusetts during very exciting times. As a young slave in the house of Colonel **John Ashley**, Freeman heard the frequent family discussions of a possible freedom from British rule. As the tension between the colonists and the British continued to grow, and **Thomas Jefferson**'s **Declaration of Independence** became the topic of everyone's conversation, Elizabeth Freeman became convinced that she too was free.

In 1781, Freeman, deciding to prove her theory, ran away from the Ashley home and contacted a young lawyer named **Theodor Sedgwick**. She explained that since th signing of the Declaration of Independenc and the passage of the **Massachusetts Co stitution**, she too was a free woma Though she knew it was dangerous, sh refused to return. Sedgwick was won ov by Freeman's argument and agreed to re resent her in court.

That same year, the county court in Gre Barrington, Massachusetts heard such ele quent statements from both Freeman an Sedgwick, that not only was Elizabeth Free man granted her freedom, but based on th state constitution, slavery was declared ill

gal. Elizabeth Freema was given thirty shilling in damages from the Ash ley family, as ordered b the judge, and went work for the Sedgwic family. Earning her ow living as a free woman, sh stayed on until her death 1829.

Because of Freeman courage and commitmen slavery was outlawed the state of Massachusett and later in the rest of th nation. It was women an men like Elizabeth Free man and Theodore Sed wick who finally validate the Declaration of Indepe dence in the United State Without them to begin th fight for equality, th essential truth of the docu ment might have been los

Elizabeth Freeman.

Phillis Wheatley, a celebrated poet until her untimely death, was born in Africa, and stolen by slave traders at the age of seven or eight. Deposited in rags from a slave ship in Boston, she was purchased by **John Wheatley** as a companion for his wife **Susannah**.

From the beginning, Phillis was a great lover of words. Susannah taught her to read and write, and within a year and a half, Phillis Wheatley was a fluent master of the English language. At 14, after devouring all the books she could find, (preferring **Alexander Pope** above all others), Phillis Wheatley wrote her first poem, which historian **Lerone Bennett** called "a blank verse eulogy of Harvard University." Printed in Boston in 1770, it was to begin her life as an internationally celebrated writer.

In 1772, due to her frail health, the Wheatleys freed Phillis and sent her to England, where she was hailed as a prodigy. Her book, *Poems on Various Subjects, Religious and Moral*, was published, with a forward signed by men such as **John Hancock**, and Phillis was invited to meet the queen. But word reached her that Susannah was ill, and Phillis returned to Boston at once. Susannah Wheatley died in 1774, and Phillis remained at the Wheatley house to care for John, never ceasing to write.

In 1775, she wrote a poem in honor of the new commander in chief of the American Army, General **George Washington**. When Washington received the poem, he sent a letter of thanks that praised the work as "elegant" and "striking," while also stating that it was only for fear of appearing vain that he did not publish it himself. Phillis was then invited to Cambridge, where she was entertained by the Washington family.

Though Phillis Wheatley moved freely as a poet, like **Lucy Terry Prince**, the first African-American to publish poetry, she had to face the severity of racism.

After the death of John Wheatley, Phillis Wheatley married a gentleman named **John Peters** who turned out to be a poor match for her. The last few years of Phillis Wheatley's life were spent in ill health and desperate poverty. The couple lost their first and second child and Phillis was working in a boarding house as a charwoman when she and her third child died within hours of one another.

Though Phillis Wheatley's death was tragic, her poems were great celebrations of freedom, Christianity, and the lives of great men. They have became part of the respected body of literature that survives to illuminate the lives and spirits of early Americans.

Phillis Wheatley.

11

5. PAUL CUFFE
1759-1817

Paul Cuffe was the founder of the African nation of **Liberia**, the first free nation in Africa employing the principles of Western countries. He was born free on Cuttyhunk Island in Massachusetts. His father was a former slave who married a Wampanoag Native American woman, and together they raised a boy who, by the age of 16, had left home to earn his living by the sea. Cuffe was well-suited to this life, and became wealthy from the success of his fishing, whaling and shipping expeditions. His fleet of 10 ships sailed to both the European and African continents regularly.

Though he was a wealthy and powerful businessman in America, Cuffe believed that only in Africa could he live truly free from racism, which had not ceased even after the **American Revolution**. In 1778, with the signing of the **Massachusetts Constitution**, Cuffe and all other African-Americans, as well as all Native Americans in Massachusetts, lost their right to vote. It was an indignity that abolitionists could not accept quietly.

Paul Cuffe.

In response, Cuffe stopped paying taxes. He argued that African-Americans and Native Americans were on the front lines of the Revolutionary War with all other Americans. They were buying their country with their lives. In 1783, a Massachusetts court voted in agreement with Cuffe and his supporters, and reinstated voting rights to all free, tax-paying African-Americans.

This victory was the first political one for Paul Cuffe, who went on to build a school on his farm for the children of his community before launching the plan that earned him the name "Father of the Black Back-to-Africa Movement."

In 1810, Cuffe made his first trip to **Sierra Leone** in Africa with the purpose of founding an African-American colony that would support itself through trade with the United States. Five years later, he traveled back with 38 of the first settlers of a new country. Once the **American Colonization Society** convinced Congress to acquire African lands for the settlement of free African-Americans, the country of Liberia, named for "liberty," was founded. (The American Colonization Society, founded by white slave owners, was an organization dedicated to moving free African-Americans to African colonies in order to deflect their attention from the abolitionist movement in America).

Though over 14,000 Americans returned to Africa over the next 30 years, many of Cuffe's contemporaries, including **Richard Allen** (see no. 6) and **Absalom Jones** stayed to protect the roots of the African-American community fighting for freedom in America.

RICHARD ALLEN
1760-1831

Richard Allen, who would found one of the first African-American Christian churches, was born in Philadelphia, but sold to the Stockley family of Delaware along with the rest of his family. An extremely bright child, Allen taught himself to read and write. He worshiped at Methodist church meetings, and at the age of 23, with the money he earned as a day laborer, purchased his freedom and began traveling with a minister who taught him to preach.

By the age of 26, he had returned to Pennsylvania, and had begun holding prayer meetings. Like other Methodists, Allen and his friend **Absalom Jones** worshiped at **St. George's Methodist Episcopal Church** in the city. Within a year of Allen's arrival in Philadelphia, St. George's had become so popular that the church ruled that black congregationalists must retreat to the back of the gallery. Absalom Jones was asked to move during prayer and forcibly pulled from his knees when he asked if the prayers could be concluded first. Rather than endure such treatment, Jones, Allen and the rest of the African-American congregation left St. George's and formed the **Free African Society**. This event inspired Allen to found his own church where African-Americans could worship freely.

Through laboring as a shoemaker, Allen bought a plot of land and began construction. By 1794, the **Bethel African Methodist Episcopal Church (AME)** was complete. Allen was named its first bishop.

Attracting a huge congregation, the AME grew past its borders, severing its ties with the Methodist Church and uniting with other African Methodist churches. Soon the expanded congregation included thousands of members united under one national organization. The church thus became the foundation of the African-American community, providing a training ground for black leadership and unifying efforts opposing slavery and racial discrimination.

Churches have remained an invaluable institution in African-American communities because of the work of men like Allen and Jones, who counted freedom of religion among the highest rights of men.

Richard Allen.

James Forten, who was a wealthy businessman and abolitionist instrumental in opposing the forcible deportation of African-Americans, grew up the son of free parents in Philadelphia. He left his family at the age of 15 to become a powder boy during the **American Revolution**. When his ship was captured by the British, not only did Forten refuse to denounce his country in return for his freedom, he gave his one chance to escape to a younger boy and stayed in captivity until a prisoner exchange was arranged.

This same tenacity made Forten a valuable employee to **Robert Bridges**, a sailmaker in Philadelphia who named Forten a foreman over 40 men within two years. When Bridges passed away, Forten purchased the business, made it one of the city's most profitable, and invented a new sailmaking device that earned him great respect, as well as wealth.

As a popular community businessman, Forten was one of the strongest voices against the forced colonization of African-Americans. When the **American Colonization Society**, made up primarily of white slave owners, attempted to pass legislation deporting all free African-Americans to Africa, Forten spoke out. He gave a speech at the **Bethel Church** in Philadelphia, stating that it was their ancestors who had enriched the land with their blood and sweat. Forten believed that African-Americans had to stay and continue to fight for freedom within their new country, and with this statement, he gained an enormous following within his community.

Forten's support for African-Americans did not stop there. He supported **Absolom Jones** and **Richard Allen** (see no. 6) by vacating the St George Church in protest, and protested Pennsylvania's attempt to restrict African American immigration from the South. He pledged both his wealth and his name to his ideals, and went on to found the **Pennsylvania Augustine Society** "for the education of people of colour." He also authored an influential text entitled *A Series of Letters by a Man of Color*.

Forever fighting for the improved position of African-Americans in America Forten unfortunately didn't live to see the end of slavery, though his words prove that he never doubted its coming: "The spirit of freedom is marching with rapid strides and causing tyrants to tremble .... May America awake...."

James Forten.

John Russwurm and his partner, **Samuel Cornish**, founded the first black newspaper in America in 1827. *The Freedom Journal*, the first record to emerge and develop as a written chronicle of black America, was the prototype for other influential papers. *Colored America* was first printed in 1837, and *The North Star* was published by **Frederick Douglass** (see no.) in 1847.

Linking people in various African-American communities, *The Freedom Journal* was the first paper to bring to light the details of lynchings, to disseminate abolitionist news, and to link America to Africa reporting on social conditions on that continent as well.

To clarify the intent of their publication, Russwurm and Cornish proclaimed their goals in their first editorial: "The publication of this journal; the expediency its appearance at this time, when so many schemes are in action concerning our people — encourage us to come boldly before an enlightened publick (sic). For we believe that a paper devoted to the dissemination of useful knowledge among our brethren, and to their moral and religious improvement, must meet with the cordial approbation of every friend of humanity.... We wish to plead our own cause. Too long have others spoken for us. Too long has the publick (sic) been deceived by misrepresentations in things which concern us dearly...."

Cornish and Russwurm lived by the same ideals that inspired their readers. Working tirelessly for the rights of all Americans, they used their journal and their lives to hasten the abolition of slavery and educate great men and women. Linked throughout the world on issues of rights and freedoms within African and African-American populations, their readers grew into a unified front that would eventually lead to freedom for all.

Samuel E. Cornish & John Russwurm.

9. DRED SCOTT
1795-1858

Dred Scott, a slave who sued for his freedom and saw his case all the way to the **US Supreme Court**, began life under the ownership of **Peter Blow** of Southampton County, Virginia. After Blow's death, Dred Scott was sold to a US Army surgeon named **John Emerson**. Emerson and his wife traveled to Fort Armstrong in Illinois and took Scott with them, though Illinois had already abolished slavery. From there, the Emersons and Scott traveled to Wisconsin, another free state, and again Scott was illegally kept, under Emerson's assertion that he was a resident of Missouri who was only temporarily traveling under the command of the US Army.

Without resistance, the Emersons too Scott back to Missouri in 1839. Mr. Eme son died in 1843 and Dred Scott attempte to buy his freedom from Mrs. Emerso When she refused to free him and his fam ly, Scott sued, claiming that for years he been enslaved in free states and should no be granted the freedom he'd been due yea earlier.

Though he lost the first case, Scott pers vered, taking his case to a second court in S Louis. This time he won, only to have tl ruling overturned by the **Missouri Suprem Court** in 1852, two years after the St. Lou court had handed him the right to freedom

To support the next and final case, Dr Scott accepted the help friends, family and white abo tionists who prepared him f the United States Suprem Court.

This ruling was the most b ter. The US Supreme Cou denied Scott the rights of American citizen, and therefo the right to sue. On March 1857, Judge **Roger B. Tan** ruled that slaveowners and the property could travel free through any state. All anti-sla ery laws were declared unco stitutional, and Dred Scott di two years later in Missouri.

To many, Scott's case w the last straw. Those who believed that slavery could abolished without violen were convinced otherwise. Tl backlash was extreme, a Scott's case strengthened tl commitment to freedom th finally pushed America in civil war, the war held respon ble for the abolition of slave nationwide.

Dred Scott.

Born in Hurley, New York, as **Isabella Baumfree**, **Sojourner Truth** was sold four times before she ran away permanently in 1826. Always passionate, Isabella went to New York City, where she worked and followed her strong religious impulses into various groups and cults, including one publicly disgraced for its questionable moral practices.

But in 1843, Isabella Baumfree went through a transition that left her forever the committed advocate of justice for all men and women. A voice from God told her, in her own words, "to travel up and down the and showing the people their sins and being a sign unto them." God told her to take the name Sojourner, and when she asked for a second name, she was told to take Truth, for she would be bringing the truth about slavery, religion, and women's suffrage to the American public for the rest of her life.

A gutsy, bold and dynamic speaker, Truth traveled throughout the country, gaining the attention of some of the brightest minds dedicated to the abolition of slavery. Though illiterate, Truth had a fanaticism and a presence that was unshakable. She was bold enough to chastise **Frederick Douglass** (see no. 14), inspire awe in **Harriet Beecher Stowe**, and shame slaveowners who tried to oppose her. She had "power and a quick, incisive mind that reduced things to their essentials," as **Lerone Bennett** said and, as Stowe said, "an unconscious superiority."

Though her focus was always on teaching the truth, her courage led her to action as well. The money she made by lecturing and singing went to African-American soldiers at the beginning of the **Civil War**, and when newly freed slaves suffered through the transition, she went to Arlington, Virginia to help them move easily into their own lives.

She was also the original freedom rider. In 1865, when Congress voted to end segregation, Truth was the first to force the subject with horse car drivers. When they refused to stop for her, she went into the middle of the street, waving her arms and demanding "I want to ride! I want to ride!" When a crowd gathered to support her, the next car was forced to stop. Truth climbed aboard and sat like stone, refusing to budge when the conductor tried to throw her off. Failing to remove her, he gave in, but Truth made sure he was later arrested and fired from his job. Once again, she had forced the point of desegregation into the lives of Americans.

She continued roaming and teaching until the end of her life. At that time, she was still trying to purchase enough land in the new western territories to support freed slaves ready to build new lives.

Sojourner Truth.

17

Nat Turner, the man who led the 1831 slave uprising, was born to an African born slave of such self-determination that she felt she could not bear to bring another slave into the world. It was said that she had to be held away from hurting him.

Along with her hate for slavery, Turner's mother also passed on a respect for religion and ritual. From childhood, Nathaniel Turner was a deeply religious person who felt he was chosen by God for a special purpose. Dedicated to prayer and the visions and voices that stirred him, Nat grew into a powerful community leader, and a commanding, learned man. In the service of a religious life, Turner denied himself all vice and stayed apart from society. Eventually, a mixture of awe and curiosity led people to call him "**the Prophet**."

Nat Turner.

In 1831, the Prophet received a vision. He is said to have heard a voice that told him to "arise and prepare myself and slay my enemies with their own weapons." After years of faithfully preaching to his community, Nat Turner gathered four men around him and began to plan the rebellion that stands as one of the most meaningful events on the road to the abolition of slavery.

At the appearance of the promised sign, the solar eclipse of February, 1831, Nat Turner and his men gathered to plot their rebellion. Through interruptions and postponements, it was stifled until the appearance of the second sign: a bluish haze over the sun in August of 1831. At that time, they decided they could wait no longer. By God's sign they entered the house of Turner's master and murdered him and his family. This was the first act of a rebellion that would kill 57 whites in 24 hours and attract 70 rebels who terrified the entire white population for months after.

On their way to Jerusalem, Virginia Turner met his first opposition. Nat's men were defeated and scattered, and Nat went into hiding for two months, eluding capture and intensifying a terror that rolled into hysteria over the eastern and southern states.

While Nat Turner hid, whites gathered in heavily armed groups, and attacked armed unarmed and innocent African-American families. Nat Turner was finally caught and brought to trial, where he pleaded "not guilty" and was sentenced to death. He predicted the sun would not shine on the day of his execution, and a surprising thunder storm rose up and swept across the sun as Turner hung from a rope in Jerusalem, Virginia.

Though the bloodshed was massive, Nat Turner managed to give a reality to the passion of black Americans who were fighting to abolish slavery in America. Nat Turner was an example of resistance and a sign to white America that freedom was imperative and would come for them one way or another.

Martin R. Delany, called "the father of black nationalism," was the son of a free woman in Charles Town, West Virginia. One of his great grandfathers had been a chief, and another a prince in their native Africa. He published his own journal, *The Mystery*, in 1847, before joining **Frederick Douglass** (see no. 14). Co-editors of *The North Star* newspaper, Delany and Douglass printed a statement of their beliefs in 1847: "It is evident we must be our own representatives and advocates, not exclusively, but peculiarly — not distinct from, but in connection with our white friends. In the grand struggle for liberty and equality now waging, it is meet, right and essential that there should arise in our ranks authors and editors, as well as orators...."

Martin R. Delany.

Douglass and Delany's ideology rested on the hope that white Americans were capable of assessing African-Americans honestly once they shared the same intellectual positions. They waited for a day when black men and women would lift themselves to positions equal to those of earned and respected white Americans.

Delany, whose pride and dignity became the foundation of his politics, went to **Harvard Medical School** in 1850, and emerged one of the most powerful antebellum influences in America. His politics shifted, as evidenced in his book, *The Condition, Elevation, Emigration and Destiny of the Colored People of the United States, Politically Considered*, which was self-published in 1853.

He claimed with great eloquence that since African-Americans had not written their own history or made their own choices, their characters were still hidden.

Delany therefore urged African-Americans to move to eastern Africa where the hard work of building a free society would bring out their strongest talents.

In 1859, Delany visited **Liberia** (see no. 5) and began an emigration campaign, which he abandoned when the **Civil War** made it possible for African-Americans to achieve respect by serving equally in the armed forces. In a letter to War Secretary **Edwin Stanton**, Delany said "We will be ready and able to raise a regiment....This is one of the measures in which the claims of the black man may be officially recognized...."

Delany entered local politics after the war, only reconsidering emigration in the late 1870s. Though he and Frederick Douglass differed in their ideologies, both believed that freedom was worth all risk, whether it be here in America, or in a new country in Africa.

Henry Garnet, whose highly influential "**Address to the Slaves of the United States**" united a whole generation of abolitionists, was himself born a slave in Kent County, Maryland. At 10 he escaped with his family to New Hope, Pennsylvania and was trained as an abolitionist and a theologian in New York. His career began early. He applied to the **Noyes Academy** in Canaan, New Hampshire with three other African-American students, and caused such violent protest that the school shut down.

His gift for oration was discovered during his address at the **American Anti-Slavery Convention** in 1840. By 1843, he was a master. At the **National Convention of Colored Citizens** in Buffalo, New York, Garnet's famous address, later called Garnet's "Call to Rebellion," proved he had grown into one of the most influential speakers of his age: "Think how many tears you have poured out upon the soil which you have cultivated with unrequited toil and enriched with your blood; and then go to your lordly enslavers and tell them plainly, that you are determined to be free....There is not much hope of redemption without the shedding of blood. If you must bleed, let it all come at once — rather die freemen, than live to be slaves."

His words struck cleanly into the hearts of the 70 delegates who had come from all over to address the issue of abolition. In a time of confusion and indeterminate activity, Garnet stated the price one must be willing to pay for freedom, and in so doing, motivated an entire generation. Though members like **Frederick Douglass** (see no. 14) opposed his revolutionary tone, Garnet's words were published with **David Walker's** *Appeal* and distributed. The eloquence of his commitment urged people to follow their passion towards the final annihilation of slavery in America.

While Garnet believed that slavery wa "the highest crime against God and man," he came to believe that total freedom wa possible only on African land. He and hi supporters were further convinced by th demoralizing passage of the 1850 **Fugitiv Slave Act**, which helped slave owner regain possession of runaways who ha escaped north.

By 1881, Garnet had embraced the ide of emigration and was made the minister o **Liberia**, a position he held for one yea before his death in 1882. Though Garne called for complete revolt in his mos famous address, he spoke from the positio of a theologian, a man devoted to the idea of Christianity. Through the network of uni fied churches, people came to hear the word of men like Garnet, and to commit their live to the creation of a wholly free society.

Henry Garnet.

20

Frederick Douglass,
rhaps the most influen-
.l man of his century,
ıs born into great pover-
Born on an unknown
te of an unknown
ther, Douglass lived on
Maryland plantation
th his mother, who was
nt to a plantation 12
iles away each day. She
uld occasionally walk
me in time to see him
bed, but she died when
ıuglass was only about
ven years old.

Frederick Douglass.

Impoverished, hungry
d parentless, Frederick struggled to sur-
ve, until the day he captured the attention
his master's daughter. **Lucretia Auld**
d Douglass sent to Baltimore as her
phew's companion, where he learned to
ad and write before Lucretia's death left
m without an ally. Without her influence,
ıuglass was sent back to the plantation,
d then to Baltimore to work the ship-
rds. There he met his future wife, **Anna**
urray, a free woman who used her nine
ars worth of savings to pay for Douglass'
ccessful escape to New York.

Once in New York, he was introduced to
illiam Lloyd Garrison, and together they
engthened black resistance. Douglass was
popular speaker who mesmerized audi-
ces with tales of his life in Maryland. He
ally wrote *The Narrative of the Life of
ederick Douglass, An American Slave* to
nvince doubters who said he was far too
ıquent and mannered to have suffered the
te he explained.

With publication came recognition, and
ıuglass, who was constantly in fear of
ıve hunters, went to England as a lecturer.
ıe eloquence of his speeches won him
ımediate support and he was encouraged to
stay on indefinitely, but
Douglass' commitment to
African-Americans still in
captivity forced him to
return to America. His
English supporters were so
concerned about him that
they bought his freedom,
allowing him to return
safely to the United States.

It was after his return to
New York in 1847 that
Douglass began publish-
ing the famous *North
Star*, named for the light
that guided slaves through
the night to safety. One of
the most influential publications in history,
The North Star, true to its name, united a
generation of abolitionists and helped guide
African-Americans toward a safer future.

Along with *The North Star*, Douglass
used his skills as an orator and diplomat to
influence American politics. As the **Civil
War** developed, it was Douglass who convinced President **Abraham Lincoln** to
free all slaves immediately so that they
might enlist in the Union forces. The
Emancipation Proclamation was issued,
and Douglass became one of the main
recruiters of free African-Americans in the
Northern territories. At the end of the Civil
War, Douglass saw a lifetime commitment
rewarded with the abolition of slavery in
America.

Until his death in 1895, Douglass continued to focus on the problems of segregation
and lynchings. He joined the crusade of
Mary Church Terrell (see no. 28) and **Ida
Wells-Barnett** (see no. 27) and maintained
his reputation as "the foremost leader of the
nineteenth century." Also called "the father
of the civil rights movement," Frederick
Douglass remains a model for new generations of American heroes.

15. HARRIET TUBMAN
1820-1913

Harriet Tubman, perhaps the most inspirational of all abolitionists, was born into slavery in Dorchester County, Maryland. Uneducated and enslaved, it was her strong religious zeal (including visions and voices) that convinced her she would one day be free. At 13, after suffering a severe blow to her head while trying to intervene between a fleeing slave and his master, Harriet began to think continually about freedom.

She married a free black man named **John Tubman**, but he did not follow her when she finally escaped north at the age of 25. She followed the north star, as hundreds did after her, to Philadelphia. She came with her fiery religious faith and a philosophy that would sustain her through unequaled acts of courage: "There was one or two things I had a right to, liberty or death; if I could not have one, I would have the other; for no man should take me alive; I should fight for my liberty as long as my strength lasted, and when the time come for me to go, the Lord would let them take me."

In Philadelphia, Tubman heard about the **Underground Railroad** and became its most famous "conductor." First, though she was already safe and employed in the North, she headed south and gathered up her sister **Mary Ann Bowley** and Mary's two children and led them through the secret channel of "safe houses" to Philadelphia.

This was the first of 19 trips. Over her years on the railroad, using old spiritual songs to hide code words, carrying a gun to encourage tired travelers to continue, opium to still crying babies, and prayers that called counsel from the sky, Harriet Tubman brought over 300 people to freedom.

Her courage was so solid that **Frederick Douglass** (see no. 14) wrote in a letter, "The difference betwee us is very marked. Most that I have do and suffered in the service of our cause h been in public....You, on the other han have labored in a private way. I ha wrought in the day — you in the night....T midnight sky and the silent stars have be the witness of your devotion to freedom a of your heroism."

Tubman's heroism continued far aft the **Emancipation Proclamation**. S tended wounded soldiers during the **Ci War**, acted as a spy, and helped newly fre slaves adjust to their new citizenship. S was a scout and personal assistant to Ge eral **Montgomery**, and founder of the **Ha riet Tubman Home for the Aged**. S raised money for the education of form slaves and participated in the **New Engla Anti-Slavery Society** with **Susan Anthony**. She died in her own retireme home of pneumonia at the age of 93.

Harriet Tubman.

Henry McNeal Turner was born the son of free parents in South Carolina. Reportedly, the family's freedom was granted by British law, which honored African loyalty and had freed the African prince from whom the family was descended.

Henry McNeal Turner believed in the rights of all men, and held that they must mold the world in which they lived. He taught himself to read and write by studying with spelling, history and law books, but his main tool was the Bible. Like many leaders before and after him, Turner found a voice that could encourage and command. That voice was nurtured by religion.

After his conversion to Chrisanity in 1851, and his subsequent censing by the white **Methodist Episcopal Church**, Turner began to preach. During his sermons, he called on men and women to enter into all facets of society alongside white Americans, and he assured them that their voices deserved to be heard: "Thousands of white people in this country are ever and anon advising the colored people to keep out of politics....If the Negro is a man in keeping with other men, why should he be less concerned about politics than anyone else? Strange too, that a number of would-be colored leaders are ignorant and debased enough to proclaim the same foolish jargon...."

Turner was also an invaluable voice in favor of the reformation of Christianity. Like **Absalom Jones** and **Richard Allen** (see no. 6), he supported the idea of an **African Methodist Episcopal Church**. Preaching for the creation of "a black God," Turner forced people to face that even their religion glorified a white man.

Henry McNeal Turner.

Not only did Turner speak about the integration of politics and religion, he actively participated in their reformation. He organized freed slaves for the **Republican Party**, and was elected a state legislator in 1867, though he was opposed by the new white **Democratic** legislators, who barred him from assuming his position. Turner was a wonderful speaker, and when he brought his case forward, claiming "I shall neither fawn nor cringe before any party, nor stoop to beg them for my rights....I am here to demand my rights...." he was returned to his seat, along with all other African-American legislators who'd been denied their positions after election.

After only one term, Turner turned from politics to the African Methodist Episcopal Church, and to the position of president of **Morris Brown College** in Georgia, where he continued to inspire a sense of pride and religious faith in his students.

Pinckney Benton Stewart Pinchback was denied his elected seat in the **US Senate** in 1873, though he was easily one of the most highly respected men of the era. He grew up in Macon, Georgia, and when his father, a white planter, died, his mother and siblings were denied any money from his estate. To help support his family, Pinchback went to work on the Mississippi riverboats.

He joined the **Union Army** at the start of the **Civil War** and was sent to recruit African-American soldiers, which he did until the army's discriminatory practices led him to quit. A great idealist, Pinchback took on the issues of universal suffrage, free public schools, and civil rights for all Americans. He joined the **Republican Party** in Louisiana, was elected to the State Senate in 1868, and founded his newspape[r] *The New Orleans Louisianian*, in 1870.

Pinchback was elected lieutenant gove[r]nor in 1871, and when Governor **Henr[y] Clay Warmoth** was impeached, Pinchbac[k] was acting governor until he was replaced i[n] January, 1873. In the same year, he wa[s] elected congressman-at-large and US Sena[tor]. The elections were immediately contest[ed], and Pinchback stood to defend himsel[f]: "....Several Senators...think me a very ba[d] man....I am bad because I have dared on se[v]eral important occasions to have an indepe[n]dent opinion. I am bad because I have dare[d] at all times to advocate and insist on exa[ct] and equal justice to all mankind...."

Though his eloquence was breathtakin[g] and his argument sound, P.B.S. Pinchbac[k] was never granted his seat in the Senat[e.] Challenged and defeated by [a] senate vote of 32 to 29, P.B.[S.] Pinchback left politics perma[]nently and returned to jou[r]nalism. In 1875, he becam[e] chairman of the **Conventio[n] of Colored Newspaper Me[n]** in Cincinnati. Speaking wi[th] great authority, he reminde[d] African-Americans of th[e] power they could wield as [a] coalition: "With this force a[s] a political element, as labo[r]ers, producers and co[n]sumers, we are an element [of] strength and wealth too pow[]erful to be ignored...."

Pinchback's leadership [at] the convention was one [of] the prime ingredients in th[e] formation of the **Associate[d] Negro Press**. He continue[d] until the end of his life t[o] influence the greatest peop[le] working in the fields of pol[i]tics and the media.

P.B.S. Pinchback.

ROBERT SMALLS
1839-1915

Robert Smalls, who proved himself one of the most courageous men of the Civil War, is well-known for one act of bravery against the Confederate Army. Smalls began the war as a slave crew member on a dispatch ship called the *Planter*. An excellent sailor and devoted to the ideal of freedom, Smalls believed that risking his life and the lives of his family on the night of May 13, 1862 was the only possible chance to secure their freedom.

The *Planter*'s officers had taken their men to shore at Charleston, South Carolina after a day of hard labor. Robert Smalls, then 23 years old, finding the ship's captain absent, arranged for his family and five others to sneak on board during the night. Smalls took on the captain's position and guided the *Planter* out into the channel with its eight person crew. The eyes of Confederate guards were upon him.

Smalls went on deck wearing Captain Relyea's characteristic straw hat and stood with his arms crossed over his chest as the ship glided past the guards. By the time they realized he wasn't Relyea, he had passed them and headed straight for Union territory.

The Confederates immediately notified Morris Island, which stood in Smalls' path, but he piloted the *Planter* out of guns' reach and prayed that Union forces wouldn't mistake him for an enemy. If they misunderstood, they might fire on the incoming ship.

Luckily for Smalls and his family, the Yankee soldiers didn't fire. Sailing carefully into the safety of Union territory, Smalls deposited the *Planter* into Union hands and joined the Union forces. Congress rewarded Smalls' amazing courage by offering him and his crew one-half of the ship's value as a reward. Smalls was also made a captain in the navy and given control of the *Planter* for the remainder of the war.

His courage became legendary, leading to the circulation of a popular story wherein two men were overheard arguing together. The first said, "Smalls, Smalls, that's all you talk about. Smalls isn't God, you know." "Sure," the second man said, "but don't forget, Smalls is young yet!"

Gaining a popular following for his support of African-American education and opportunity, Robert Smalls took up politics. He was elected to the South Carolina House of Representatives, the state senate, and the US Congress, where he pursued equal opportunity legislation.

Robert Smalls.

Elijah McCoy is one of the success stories of the **Underground Railroad**. His parents were slaves in Kentucky who took their lives into their own hands and escaped through the tunnels and tributaries that flowed towards the North Star. Arriving in Canada, they built a family of twelve children, one of whom was destined to make the name McCoy a household word.

Elijah was educated in Edinburgh, Scotland, where he became fascinated with the study of mechanical engineering. Moving from there back to the states, Elijah settled in Detroit, Michigan, in hopes of finding work. Though he was an inventive engineer, prejudice made it impossible for him to find a position except as a fireman for the **Michigan Central Railroad**.

This turned out to be the position that inspired him. After watching the inefficient machinery of the contemporary trains, and the daily oiling of all working parts, Elijah founded the **Elijah McCoy Manufacturing Company** in Detroit and began working on the production of a device that would oil machinery even while the piece was still in motion. In 1872, his new "lubricator cup"

received a **US patent** and began to stream line the steam engine, saving operators valuable time and money.

Though he had perfected a device that became invaluable, Elijah McCoy was not satisfied. He went to work on a variation and perfected over 42 inventions that modernized machinery all over the world.

A lifetime inventor and perfectionist Elijah McCoy remained the specialist the people trusted, and when copies were offered to prospective buyers, they would say, "I want the **Real McCoy**."

Elijah McCoy.

Howard Latimer.

Howard Latimer, the creator of the **Latimer Lamp**, was born in Chelsea, Massachusetts, where he was allowed to go to school only until he was 10 years old. When his father left the family in 1858, Lewis quit school and went to work for a legal firm, **Crosby & Gould**, that specialized in drafting illustrations for inventions waiting to be patented. Though Latimer was hired as an office boy, his interest in the trade led him to purchase a second-hand set of drafting tools. With library books and through friends in the firm, Latimer taught himself the craft of drafting.

Latimer's superb drawings earned him the position of junior draftsman, and he was quickly promoted to chief draftsman. Then, when Latimer met **Alexander Graham Bell**, a friendship formed and Bell asked for drawings of his new invention, the telephone. When Bell applied for the patent in 1876, it was Latimer's drawings that he presented.

In 1880, Latimer went to work for the **United States Electric Lighting Company** in Connecticut. His fascination with the detail and mechanics of drafting was the same heartfelt interest that he applied to the invention of his own lamp. After learning about the new process of electric lighting, he went to work on inventing improved filaments. He was so successful in the production of the new "Latimer Lamp," that he was then hired to oversee the building of the New York electric light plants. He was also sent to England by **Maxim-Weston Electric Company** to build an incandescent light division.

It was in 1884, after he'd worked with some of the age's greatest inventors, that Latimer was asked to join a small, elite group of crackerjack inventors called the **Edison Pioneers**. Working closely with **Thomas Edison**, this group came to the forefront of the contemporary age of discovery. Latimer continued with the project to the end of his life.

George Washington Williams, who was a politician, journalist, historian and fearless soldier, was one of America's finest renaissance men. He began his first career by lying to the army in order to join the **6th Massachusetts Regiment** at the age of 14. Williams was discovered, returned to civilian life, and reenlisted as a sergeant major two years later. Fearless in combat, Williams was wounded for the first time near Fort Harrison, Virginia, in 1864. He was discharged in 1865, when he promptly joined the Mexican army. He resigned a year later and joined the US Army's 10th Cavalry, under whose service he was wounded a second time during a campaign against the **Comanche Indians** of the western plains.

This time, he accepted a medical discharge and changed careers. The second skill in a long list of those he mastered was theology. Williams graduated from the **Newton Theological Institute** in Massachusetts in 1874 and served as an ordained minister in Boston for a year before moving to Washington, DC.

Williams finally chose his life work when he began writing and publishing an influential newspaper called *The Commoner*. Men like **Frederick Douglass** (see no. 14) put their support behind it, and though the paper eventually went under, Williams continued to write for several other papers while he took up the study of law. In 1879, he was elected to the **Ohio legislature**, and began to collect the details of African-American lives. His collection grew to encompass two volumes entitled *History of the Negro Race From 1619 to 1880*. Published in 1883, it received enormous praise for the depth of its research. Like everything Washington pursued, this book was an excellent piece of work, and it stood alone as one of the great histories of American life.

After five years, Williams published his second book, *History of the Negro Troops*

George Washington Williams.

in the War of Rebellion. The success of both books made Williams a popular speaker who was often invited to lecture throughout Europe. After he'd been in Belgium one year, Williams was convinced by King **Leopold II** to help develop the **Congo Free State** in Africa. Williams was so interested that he went to visit this supposed free state which was, in fact, owned by the King. Not only were the Congolese people under the jurisdiction of King Leopold, but the workers were treated like slaves.

The conditions he found were so shocking and demoralizing that Williams wrote *An Open Letter to His Serene Majesty Leopold II, King of the Belgians*, in which he denounced the cruelty and inhumanity of the king's Congolese colony. With this and two more reports, Williams raised international interest in the Congo. He went on to research the Portuguese and British colonies in the rest of the continent.

Though he died very young, his life had been spent in the service of justice and community, and millions of lives were effected by his passion.

Cowboy **Nat Love**, also known as Deadwood Dick from his autobiography entitled *The Life and Times of Nat Love, Better Known in Cattle Country as "Deadwood Dick,"* was once a sharecropper in Tennessee. He worked hard to support his widowed mother and his sister, but when good luck came his way and granted him the winning ticket in a raffle, Love left the life of farming behind.

Selling the horse that was his prize, he gave half of the money to his mother and left for Dodge City, Kansas, where he began to live the life of legend.

There are stories about the 14 gunshot wounds that he survived, and more tales about the skill with which he could train a horse, brand a steer, and use a gun. There are stories about his wild drinking nights with his friend **Bat Masterson**, and a story in which Nat Love rode his horse through a bar and ordered a couple of drinks — one for himself and one for his horse.

He was a legendary gunfighter in his youth, and an exceptionally skilled one. During the 1876 Fourth of July celebration held in Deadwood, South Dakota, Love proved it by winning rifle and handgun matches, rope throws and a bucking bronco contest. One of the many African-American cowboys responsible for settling the wild western territory, Love fought Native Americans, moved with the railroad, and herded cattle for the **Pete Gillinger Company** in Arizona.

Even with his reputation, Love was just like any other pioneer when he left his past behind and headed west working on the railroad. Just like thousands of other bold travelers, he laid one stone on the road west. He wrote his autobiography in 1907 and was later living in Los Angeles as a **Pullman porter**. By risking everything to settle new territory, he made it possible for his family to experience freedom in America, and for many others to follow his family's example.

Nat Love.

23. TIMOTHY THOMAS FORTUNE
1856-1928

T. Thomas Fortune was an influential journalist and agitator who constantly fought for the fullest implementation of the **14th and 15th amendments**.

Born in 1856 in Marianna, Florida, Fortune grew up while African-Americans were striving hardest for the civil rights promised after the **Civil War**. His father had been a slave, but the **Emancipation Proclamation** made it possible for him to join the Florida legislature. His political influence made him a target for white Southerners who wished to cripple the **Reconstruction**, and Fortune's family finally moved to Jacksonville to avoid violent **Ku Klux Klan** threats.

T. Thomas Fortune was educated at **Freedman's Bureau schools**, and became a printer before studying law briefly at **Howard University**. He moved to New York in 1879, and was hired as a printer for the *Rumor*. By 1881, the year the *Rumor* had progressed into the *Globe*, Fortune had become editor and part-owner.

In 1884, Fortune bought his own newspaper, the *New York Freeman*, which became the *New York Age* in 1887. In the same year, his *Black and White: Land, Labor and Politics in the South* was published. It was a piece dedicated to Fortune's true passion: the unification of black and white forces for the civil rights — especially the right to vote — of all Americans, and particularly African-Americans.

His views were further articulated during an important meeting of the **National Afro-American League (NAAL)** in 1890. The 147 representatives from 21 states heard Fortune detail the battle still in progress: "As the agitation which culminated in the abolition of African slavery in this country covered a period of 50 years, so may we expect that before the rights conferred upon us by the war amendments are fully conceded, a full century will have passed away.

We have undertaken no child's play. W[e] have undertaken a serious work which wi[ll] tax and exhaust the best intelligence an[d] energy of the race for the next century...."

Fortune's newspaper became a place f[or] the open discussion of ideals held by me[n] like **Booker T. Washington** (see no. 24[).] Known for its militancy and its unwaverin[g] support of society's underprivileged clas[s]es, the *Age* was a powerful forum for Was[h]ington and his supporters against the sep[a]ratist politics of **W.E.B. Du Bois** (see n[o.] 32) and others.

Fortune remained a writer even after h[e] sold his paper in 1907. From then un[til] 1919, he wrote for the *Norfolk Journal*, an[d] in 1923, he became a controversial figu[re] once again when he became the editor [of] **Marcus Garvey**'s *Negro World* (see n[o.] 46). Garvey, called "the most dangero[us] enemy of the Negro people" by W.E.B. D[u] Bois for his "Back to Africa" policy, gav[e] Fortune his last opportunity to shape pub[lic] opinion, inspire debate and broaden futu[re] possibilities for all Americans.

T. Thomas Fortune.

Booker T. Washington.

Booker T. Washington, one of the most politically influential men to emerge from the **Reconstruction**, was born into slavery, which was abolished when he was nine years old. At the end of the **Civil War**, his mother moved him and his family to Malden, West Virginia. Washington began working at the salt mines and taught himself to read and write before setting out for **Hampton Normal & Agricultural Institute** in Virginia. An exceptional intellect, Washington rose to top of his class and graduated with honors.

Washington showed early promise as a leader and a scholar. When the 1881 Alabama legislature decided to train black teachers at a new school in Tuskegee, the head of Hampton Normal recommended that Washington develop its programs. As the **Tuskegee Institute**'s new president, Washington went to work building a leading institution out of an abandoned plantation in Alabama. His students were the architects and carpenters of classrooms, dormitories, a church, and a curriculum that included everything from farming to printing.

Tuskegee became the center of a self-motivation movement, and Washington's sphere of influence grew to include men like US presidents **William Howard Taft** and **Theodore Roosevelt**. Washington believed that a man must take responsibility for raising his own station in life. To support Tuskegee, he befriended many wealthy businessmen and many white leaders so that he might gain their support and their financial backing. This tactic led to his reputation as an accomodationist, someone who would graciously befriend the same men who had supported slavery.

This was one of the controversial sides of Washington's ideology, though with the help of white business people, Washington made it possible for African-Americans to receive the education that was critical to their survival after Reconstruction. His diplomacy was a tool for building a bridge between the separate communities, and it was the reason he was consistently invited to advise presidents and business leaders. It was also the reason that rivalries sprang up between himself and men like **W.E.B. Du Bois** (see no. 32).

Credited with the monumental success of Tuskegee, Washington is also known for the success of the **National Negro Business League**, which he founded in 1892 to support black-owned businesses. He is also remembered for the **Atlanta Compromise address**, which he gave in 1895, stating that "The enjoyment of all the privileges that will come to us must be the result of severe and constant struggle rather than artificial forcing." His story is detailed in his autobiography, *Up From Slavery*, which was not only a best seller in America, but an internationally popular text.

Though his politics were hotly debated during his life and after, there is no denying that Booker T. Washington was one of the most active supporters of African-American education. His ideals were based principally on the self-respect and the infinite potential of independent men and women.

In 1893, Dr. **Daniel Hale Williams** performed one of the world's medical miracles when he completed the first successful operation to repair a torn human heart. After years of dedication to the training and treatment of African-Americans, Williams was catapulted into a position where other leaders, including US President **Grover Cleveland**, were his admirers and his greatest allies in the foundation of African-American hospitals.

Born in Hollidaysburg, Pennsylvania, Williams left school to apprentice with a shoemaker when he was only 12. He attended **Haire's Classical Academy** in Wisconsin, and apprenticed with Dr. **Henry Palmer** before attending **Chicago Medical College**. Gaining a reputation as a quick study, Williams completed Chicago Medical in only three years.

He opened his own practice, taught at Chicago Medical College, and joined the surgical staff at **South Side Dispensary**. Proving himself a dedicated and tireless doctor, Williams was then appointed to the **Illinois State Board of Health** in 1889.

Williams was extremely sensitive to the needs of African-Americans, and the appalling lack of facilities available both for training and treatment. He founded **Provident Hospital & Training Association** in 1891 and opened it to the service of all citizens, and to the training of black students of medicine.

It was at Provident that Williams faced the dilemma that made him world famous. In an age where the damaged human heart was untreatable, Williams received **James Cornish**, a man brought to the hospital with a lethal stab wound. Without antibiotics or X rays, without any history of success, Williams managed to mend the rip in the dying man's heart. was an invaluable evolutionary leaps for modern medicine.

President Grover Cleveland acknowledged Dr. Williams by honoring him with the position of chief surgeon at **Freedman's Hospital** in Washington DC. Williams used the influence of his new position to open a second training facility for African-American doctors and nurses.

Williams continued to support the medical training and treatment of African-Americans throughout his career, and by his retirement in 1926, had helped establish over 40 new hospitals.

Dr. Daniel Hale Williams.

Granville T. Woods was an ingenious inventor born in Columbus, Ohio, where he was educated until the age of 10. He was then forced to leave school in order to help support his family. By the age of 16, Woods had already moved to Missouri where he worked as a fireman and a railroad engineer.

Later, Woods returned to his education. He moved to New York, began working as an engineer on the steamship *Ironsides*, and studied electrical engineering. Like many great men, it was a dedication to learning that inspired Woods' greatest work. In 1884 he returned to Ohio and convinced his brother **Lyates** to join him in opening a new machine shop. Focusing on telephone and telegraph technology, Woods not only sold existing mechanisms, but began to invent new ones.

In 1884 Woods won his first patent for a **telephone transmitter** so advanced that it was immediately bought by the **American Bell Telephone Company** in Boston. Next, he built a device that integrated the function of the telephone with that of the telegraph, and by 1887, had won seven more patents for machines that improved communications.

Working steadily until his death, Woods patented over 60 inventions, including a telegraph that sends messages to moving trains, the light dimmer, the electromagnetic brake, and the electrified component that allows rail cars to operate underground as subways. His inventions were highly prized by the important companies in the country. Some were bought by **General Electric**, others by **American Bell Telephone**, and still others by **Westinghouse**.

Woods could not be matched in the field of invention, but he took a great risk one year and accused a manager from the **American Engineering Company** of stealing patents. In response, the company brought a libel suit that carried on until Woods had lost nearly his entire fortune to legal fees for his defense. He died with almost nothing, except the reputation of a great inventor.

Granville T. Woods.

Ida Bell Wells, who dedicated her adult life to a successful anti-lynching campaign, was born a slave in Holly Springs, Mississippi. She grew up quickly after losing both her parents when she was only 16. Becoming the sole parent to her five siblings, she lied about her age and took a job as a teacher, supporting the entire family on $25 a month.

She moved to Missouri in 1884, continued to teach, and began writing for the *Living Way* and the *Memphis Free Speech* newspapers. When she was fired from her teaching position for protesting the poor conditions at her school, Wells took what little savings she had and bought part ownership of the *Free Speech*. Her effective reporting was responsible for increasing subscriptions by 2,000 in the first nine months.

The more Wells learned, the more committed she became, and the more enemies she created. When three black men were taken from a Memphis jail and lynched, Wells reported that the men were not perpetrators of a crime, but successful young entrepreneurs who had begun to lure customers away from a white-owned business. Uncovering the names of the city officials who refused to condemn the lynching, and those who admitted that they were in support of it, Wells caused a sensation. Her report was so damning that it convinced black citizens to refuse to use the city's

Ida B. Wells-Barnett.

expensive new streetcars as a sign of unified protest, and this boycott nearly broke the streetcar company. Wells even urged them to leave the city, and over 2,000 people moved north from Memphis in search of a just and safe society.

Ida Wells was now a celebrated journalist, and this was only the first of her investigations. She found that 1,217 African-Americans had been lynched between the years of 1890 and 1900. Her famous "**Red Record**" detailed lynchings which occurred in three of those years. Listing the victims and the official reasons for their murders, the Red Record soon became one of the most shocking documents of American history. Here was the proof that all lynchings were not related to crimes. Of the 728 lynchings she investigated, only one-third of the victims were accused of crimes. Most of these were not even tried in a court of law.

Wells continued her investigation throughout her life. Though she was repeatedly threatened, and her newspaper office was burned to the ground, she continued to research case after case from her new home in New York. She also organized women's clubs and political meetings with the help of her husband, **Ferdinand Lee Barnett**, whom she married in 1895. She supported the need for a national group of African-Americans, and was an influential founder of the **National Association for the Advancement of Colored People (NAACP)** in 1909.

Mary Church Terrell, an extremely successful advocate of women's rights — particularly black women's rights — grew up as the wealthy daughter of real estate broker **Robert Church**. He sent his daughter to **Oberlin College**, from which she graduated with a master's degree in 1888.

Mary Church Terrell was a spirited, intelligent woman who was quickly offered a position at **Wilberforce University**. In an age when wealthy women did not work, her father was scandalized, but no matter how he threatened, he did not stop her from accepting the position and encouraging other women to join academia: "He disinherited me....refused to write to me for a year because I went to Wilberforce to teach. Further, I was ridiculed and told that no man would want to marry a woman who studied higher mathematics. I said I'd take a chance and run the risk."

It was this friction that inspired Terrell to take up the issue of women's suffrage. And it was the lynching of three innocent black men in 1891 that inspired her to join the anti-lynching campaign begun by **Ida B. Wells-Barnett** (see no. 27).

One of the three victims had been a dear friend, and Church was compelled to contact **Frederick Douglass** (see no. 14) and ask his support. Together, the two of them approached US President **Benjamin Harrison** and asked that he condemn lynching in his next address to Congress. His refusal was such a bitter disappointment that Terrell was moved to a lifetime of service against lynching and all other crimes related to racism and sexism.

She married **Robert Terrell**, and immediately turned down a position as registrar at Oberlin College. A appointed to the Washington, DC Board of Education in 1895, she became the first African-American woman on the board, and her influential new associates became invaluable supporters of her lifetime campaigns, which she never laid down.

Working with **Susan B. Anthony** and **Jane Addams**, Mary Church Terrell helped the **National American Woman Suffrage Association** pass the 19th Amendment. She also taught white women suffragettes to include African-American women in their actions, even if it threatened their support from the South.

Terrell was a founder of the **Women Wage-Earners Association**, which supported black women employees. She was one of the founders of the **National Association of Colored Women (NACW)** and a founder of the **National Association for the Advancement of Colored People (NAACP)**.

Dedicated to the rights of all women, and the fair treatment of all men, Mary Church Terrell put pressure on the **American Association of University Women** to open their doors to black women, and at the age of 90 headed a picket line that pressured restaurants into desegregation.

Mary Church Terrell.

GEORGE WASHINGTON CARVER 1864-1943

George Washington Carver was a scientist whose agricultural experiments at the **Tuskegee Institute** produced over 400 new products from soil-enhancing crops. He's best known for inventing byproducts of the peanut during his nearly 50 years at Washington's university, where he was also responsible for training young African-Americans to sustain themselves in the newly-reformed United States.

Born a slave in Diamond Grove, Missouri during the **Civil War**, Carver and his mother were reportedly kidnapped by raiders in his youth. His mother disappeared, but a ransom was paid for Carver's return. After the **Emancipation** he stayed on at the **Moses and Susan Carver Plantation** and learned to read and write before attending school in Neosho, Missouri, and later, Minneapolis, Kansas.

Carver's intense interest in botany led him to **Highland University**. He was accepted on the merits of his application, but rejected when he showed up for studies and the University realized he was not white. At that time, the university did not accept African-American students.

Undaunted, Carver applied to **Simpson College** in Iowa in 1890 and was admitted. He transferred to **Iowa State University** in 1891 and graduated with honors in 1894. He joined the faculty after the completion of his master's degree and remained at Iowa State until he received an intriguing letter from **Booker T. Washington** (see no. 24). In it, Washington said, "I can't offer you money, position or fame....I offer you in their place work — hard, hard work — the task of bringing a people from degradation, poverty, and waste to full manhood."

Carver responded, "I am coming."

Carver went on to serve as director of the **Agricultural Research & Experimental Station at Tuskegee Normal & Industrial Institute** in Alabama. He was also an active

pursuer of agricultural inventions tha would replenish starved Southern lands su fering from single crop nutrient depletio after generations of tobacco and cotton pro duction. It was Carver's discovery tha legumes like peanuts could be planted fo their replenishing nutrients, and harveste for their superior oils, their richness in pro tein and their 300 byproducts, includin peanut butter, shampoo, coffee and fac powder. One year of peanuts, followed by year of cotton, not only increased the var ety of production, but increased the quali of the cotton crop.

Individually inventing over 400 produc made from the peanut and the sweet pota alone, Carver's discoveries taught a Southerners how to maximize their lan The South rose again as a pioneering, agr cultural sweet spot for the nation. In h own words, "...It has always been the on great ideal of my life to be of the greate good to the greatest number of my people.

George Washington Carver.

MATTHEW HENSON
1866-1955

Matthew Henson, the first man to see the **North Pole**, was born in Charles County, Maryland, where he lost his mother when he was only two, and his father when he was eight. He went to live with an uncle in Washington, DC, but quit school when he decided to be a sailor. Running away at the age of 12, Henson joined **Captain Child's** crew on the merchant ship *Katie Hinds*. As Child's cabin boy, Henson left Baltimore and travelled around the world for six years — over the Atlantic and Pacific oceans, into the China and Baltic seas and through the Straits of Magellan.

Henson became an expert at charting and navigating before returning to Washington, DC, where he was discovered by the explorer Admiral **Robert E. Peary**. Peary walked into a clothing store to find Henson, an expert seaman who had retired from the sea before the age of 20, now clerking in a clothing store. Impressed with the breadth of Henson's knowledge and experience, Peary invited him to join an expedition designed to investigate the feasibility of a canal linking the Atlantic and Pacific oceans through Nicaragua. Henson accepted.

The Nicaragua Expedition quickly showed Peary what an invaluable associate Henson could be. When they were home again, Peary revealed that his dream had always been to be the first man to reach the North Pole, and during their 20 year association, Peary and Henson undertook seven expeditions with this goal in mind.

Six times they were halted by the cruelest conditions, sometimes within a few hundred miles of their destination. Nevertheless, they began to plan the seventh expedition. Henson had taught himself to

Matthew Henson.

build sledges, speak the Inuit language, and master a team of dogs, so when six dog teams left Crane City, Greenland in 1908, it was with Matthew Henson in the lead.

He covered 35 miles the first day and rose early on the second to lead Peary and a team of Inuit experts towards the top of the world. On April 6, 1909, Matthew Henson arrived at the North Pole, followed by his Inuit guides and Commander Peary.

Robert Peary, whose progress was slower after losing several toes to frostbite, confirmed Henson's calculations, participated in about 30 hours of study, and planted the American flag.

It wasn't until 1945 that Henson received the **Navy Medal** from Congress, and not until 1961 that a plaque was erected in his honor at the State House at Annapolis, Maryland. In 1988, Henson's remains were moved to **Arlington National Cemetery**, where he was buried with full honors next to Robert Peary.

Sarah Breedlove was a woman who turned her inventive mind and excellent business sense into a million dollar company improving not only the quality of her own life, but also that of many African-Americans.

Breedlove's parents were both recently freed slaves who died when she was only five. She then left the Louisiana plantation where she was born and lived with her sister until marrying a man named McWilliams when she was 14. She lost him as well — to a lynch mob — when she was only 20. Left alone to raise her young daughter **A'lelia**, she went to work as a washerwoman, and like other women, sacrificed her health to take good care of her child. Poverty and bad nutrition, combined with traditional "wrap and twist" hair straightening methods, made her hair begin to thin.

Breedlove began experimenting with methods to stop hair loss and one night had a dream in which an old man gave her the ingredients for a potion that not only stopped balding, but quickened regrowth By the time she met her second husband the newspaper man **C.J. Walker**, Sara Breedlove and her relatives were alread filling jars with her **Wonderful Hair Grow er** and selling them. It was Walker wh taught her the advertising and mail orde techniques that changed her small busines into a million dollar success.

Madame C.J. Walker went on to fashio hair care products particularly designe for black hair. She developed the **hot com** and promoted the idea that beauty wa derived from cleanliness and not fron racial qualities. She opened her first beau ty school, the **Lelia College**, in Pittsburg in 1908, and managed a staff of door-to door agents who began to earn up t $1,000 a day in commissions. By 1919 25,000 agents worked for her. They taugh women how to take pride in their beautifu hair and skin while encouraging them t start their own beauty shops.

Walker's success allowed her to sen A'lelia to **Knoxville College** and to begi focusing on her own education. With inde pendent tutors, Madame Walker concentrat ed for the first time on the luxuries of a for mal education. Her respect for higher learn ing would ultimately lead her to donat money to several institutions and leader including **Tuskegee Institute** (see no. 24 and **Frederick Douglass** (see no. 14).

Throughout her life, Walker asserte that if a woman could run her own busi ness, she could certainly manage her ow life. Putting hundreds of women to work i her company and in their own beaut shops, Walker made sure that her succes promoted the success of all women lookin for means to manage their own lives. He example taught women how to pursue busi ness for themselves, appreciate their ow beauty, and take responsibility for thei own education.

Madame C.J. Walker.

W.E.B. DU BOIS
1868-1963

W.E.B. Du Bois.

William Edward Burghardt Du Bois was born in Great Barrington, Massachusetts. Through founding the **Niagara Movement** and *Crisis* magazine, and motivating innumerable leaders, Du Bois became an influential role model for generations of African-Americans. He was the first black man to graduate from **Harvard** with a Ph.D. in Social Sciences, and his doctoral dissertation, *The Suppression of the African Slave Trade*, became his first book, published in 1896.

Du Bois accepted a position as professor of history and economics at **Atlanta University**, and while there helped in the formation of the first formal black academic committee, the **American Negro Academy**. His eloquent and educational essays were published in a famous collection called *The Souls of Black Folk*, where Du Bois covered numerous issues related to race, including his negative opinion of **Booker T. Washington**'s tactics of appeasement (see no. 24) in the overwhelmingly white world of education and economics. It was also during his time at Atlanta that Du Bois and others formed the Niagara Movement (1905), an organization in direct opposition to Booker T. Washington's **Tuskegee Movement**. The Niagara Movement was based on such principles as: a militant response to all racial discrimination, the idea of complete equality between races, and the education of what Du Bois called "a talented tenth" of the Negro population who could then lead the entire population toward 'self-realization and its highest cultural possibilities." It was the Niagara Movement that grew into perhaps the most influential African-American coalition in history, the **National Association for the Advancement of Colored People (NAACP)**.

Though the conflicting ideas of Du Bois and Washington split African-American communities into separate factions, they also managed to inspire a debate that drove people to envision new futures for African-Americans in American society.

And neither man stopped there. Du Bois began to publish the monthly magazine *Crisis*, which highlighted the issues and writings of black leaders. In 1910, he left Atlanta to lead the NAACP, as director of research and publicity, and *Crisis* grew into a forum for the ideas of African-American writers and artists who would later be associated with the **Harlem Renaissance** (see no. 36), including **Langston Hughes** (see no. 64), **Marian Anderson** (see no. 63), and **Arna Bontemps**.

He was a consistently fine writer whose works include *Black Reconstruction* and *The World and Africa*. He co-founded the **Pan-African Congress** in 1919, and later became a devoted peace activist who chaired the **Peace Information Center** against the proliferation of atomic weapons.

Investigated and indicted for his relationship to a "foreign agent," in 1951 Du Bois' passport was denied. He was shunned by many of his associates and unable to continue much of his work until 1958, when the **US Supreme Court** struck down the validity of the court's original statute. Du Bois toured Asia, Europe and the Soviet Union before moving to Ghana on President **Kwame Nkrumah's** invitation, where he began to edit the *Encyclopedia Africana*. He remained in Ghana until his death.

John Hope's own words are perhaps the most telling statement of his life's work and his character: "If we are not striving for equality, in heaven's name for what are we living? I regard it as cowardly and dishonest for any of our colored men to tell white people or colored people that we are not struggling for equality....Yes, my friend, I want equality. Nothing less....If equality, political, economic, and social, is the boon of other men in this great country of ours, then equality, political, economic, and social, is what we demand....Rise, Brothers! Come let us possess this land. Never say: 'Let well enough alone.' Cease to console yourselves with adages that numb the moral sense. Be discontented. Be dissatisfied...."

John Hope's statement is particularly striking when it is understood against the background of his situation. This speech was made in Nashville in 1906, and in response to **Booker T. Washington's** Atlanta Compromise address (see no. 24). John Hope was the president of **Atlanta Baptist College** at the time, and as such, a very visible figure. In great opposition to Washington and all the powerful white supporters of his college he was also a great friend of **W.E.B. Du Bois** (see no. 32).

Hope was born in Augusta, Georgia. He'd graduated with a B.A. from **Brown University** in 1894, and taught at Atlanta Baptist College for eight years before he became president. When he stood up as president and opposed the compromises of Washington and his supporters, John Hope was declaring publicly that he held equality above all other treasures, above even the security of his career.

John Hope.

That courage made him a great ally to Du Bois and the other influential members of the **Niagara Movement**. It also made him a powerful force in the field of education. Asserting that African-Americans must enter into higher education, Hope helped shape the policies of the nation's schools by presiding over both Atlanta Baptist College and **Atlanta University** — an affiliate school that served both men and women. He also presided over both the **National Association of Teachers of Colored Schools** and the **Association for the Study of Negro Life & History**.

A man held in the highest esteem, John Hope finished his life in the service of higher learning after a lifetime of holding his peers to the ideal of equality.

Scott Joplin, considered "the King of Ragtime," was born in Texarcana, Texas where he taught himself to play piano in the houses where his mother worked as a maid. News of his talent spread through the city and soon a German music teacher picked Joplin up as a student and taught him the formalities of music.

When Joplin's mother died, he began to travel as a musician, taking note of emerging musical styles and finding a particular interest in the syncopated rhythms of **ragtime**. Based on old slave tunes, ragtime combined their soulful melodies with varied rhythm patterns, producing a fast, even sound that became the basis of a new dance craze. "Ragging the melody," which began on New Orleans river boats, swept through urban dance halls, and when Scott Joplin played it, ragtime became the signature of a generation.

Joplin moved to St. Louis in 1895 and began playing his brand of ragtime at Honest John Turpin's Silver Dollar Saloon. He then moved to Sedalia, where he took classes in music theory from **George R. Smith College**. At night, he practiced his own style at the **Maple Leaf Club**. He then began to publish his music.

In 1899, Joplin's "Oriental Rags" was published, but his next piece, the famous "Maple Leaf Rag" was rejected by two publishers before music dealer **John Stark** printed it — and watched it sell more than one million copies. The most popular piece of sheet music in publication at the time, the "Maple Leaf Rag" made ragtime an international sensation.

As ragtime's popularity soared, and Joplin's simpler rags became popular, he became entranced with a new form. Interested in achieving the musical excellence of European classics, Joplin followed his passion for artistic complexity and began writing opera. His first, *The Guest of Honor,* was not well received. Joplin began work on the next, a folk opera in honor of his mother. *Treemonisha* was such a complex and unique piece of music that Joplin could not find a producer. Deciding to risk everything, he produced the piece himself with complete faith. He then watched it close almost immediately. Joplin's audience, unimpressed and disappointed, rejected his opera at the same time that his ragtime was being replaced by a new form called **jazz**.

Joplin never recovered from the disappointment of *Treemonisha*'s failure. Committed to Manhattan State Hospital in 1916, Joplin died that spring without realizing that his music would be revived in the last half of the 20th century. "The Entertainer" became the chosen theme song for the Academy Award-winning movie *The Sting,* and his beloved opera, *Treemonisha,* was finally produced on **Broadway** in the 1970s, where it delighted contemporary audiences. Joplin remains forever and always "the King of Ragtime."

Scott Joplin.

35. ROBERT ABBOTT
1870-1940

Robert Abbott, the founder and editor of *The Chicago Defender*, was raised in Georgia by his mother and his stepfather, a man who had such a positive influence on Abbott that he took his surname, **Sengstacke**, as his middle name. It was in Sengstacke's Georgian newspaper office that Abbott learned the printing trade. He then left for Chicago, where he attended **Hampton Institute** and **Kent College of Law**.

After graduation, Abbott tried to found a practice, and ended up moving to the Midwest and working for five years before returning to Chicago in 1903. In 1905, he reportedly invested his entire savings, a total of 25 cents, into the first edition of *The Chicago Defender*. The first issue was a four page document produced at a desk in his landlady's kitchen and sold door-to-door for two cents each. These were the humble beginnings of one of America's influential black newspapers.

Dedicated to increasing the migration of African-Americans to the comparatively liberal North, *The Defender* was one of the few voices speaking honestly on black issues, educating people about lynchings, the coming machination of farming in the South, and the improved standard of living for African-Americans in the industrialized North.

The Chicago Defender was a strong supporter of the NAACP and claimed its goals as the goals of the newspaper: manhood suffrage, an end to discrimination in public accommodations, the right to socialize with all willing to socialize with them, equality under the law, and education for all children.

To these ends, Abbott published some of the best writers and thinkers on the subject of concern to black America. Though *The Defender* was sometimes banned in areas for its militancy, Abbott often supported his position with dramatic exposes on the extremity of racism, the violence and the dire economic circumstances experienced by African-Americans in both the South and the North.

Outside the newspaper, Abbott was a great activist. Serving on the **Chicago Commission of Race Relations**, he worked for the desegregation of neighborhoods and supported political candidates who fought for the inclusion of African-Americans in President **Franklin Roosevelt**'s New Deal policies.

Robert Abbott.

James Weldon Johnson, writer, musician and member of the **NAACP**, was born in Jacksonville, Florida. James attended **Atlanta University**, from which he graduated in 1894, before returning to Jacksonville, where he took the position of principal of the Stanton School until 1901.

In that year, he and his talented brother **J. Rosamond Johnson** moved to New York City, where they became musical collaborators on songs like "Since You Went Away" and "Lift Every Voice and Sing." They wrote for the stage with **Robert Cole** and saw their pieces performed on **Broadway**.

All of this was a precursor to Johnson's involvement in the **Harlem Renaissance**, which brought elements of black culture to the forefront of American culture. Along with icons **Langston Hughes** (see no. 64),

James Weldon Johnson.

Marian Anderson (see no. 63), **Claude McKay** (see no. 47) and others who were writing and performing in Harlem, James Weldon Johnson became a spokesperson for the African-American experience. He was one of the artists aware of the economic and social problems of post-war America — a time when America was celebrating peace with a lot of patriotism. With new pride and articulate voices, the writers of the Renaissance demanded the respect their obvious artistry deserved.

In 1906, Johnson was President **Theodore Roosevelt**'s choice for **US consul** in Venezuela, and in 1909 he was transferred to Nicaragua. In 1912, Johnson's career as an influential novelist began with the publication of *The Autobiography of an Ex-Colored Man*, in which he detailed the life of a black man passing for white. In 1913, he became editor for the *New York Age*, and in 1916, began to use his diplomatic experience to help the NAACP. He became the agency's secretary and oversaw the organization of new branches throughout the nation, while focusing further attention on the powerful anti-lynching campaign headed by his associate **Ida B. Wells-Barnett** (see no. 27).

With the dawn of the Harlem Renaissance, which made Harlem, New York, one of the world's exciting cultural centers of the 1920s and 30s, Johnson published extensively. *The Book of American Negro Spirituals* was published in 1925, its sequel in 1926, and *God's Trombones, Seven Negro Sermons in Verse, Black Manhattan* and *Negro American, What Now?* all before 1935.

One of the first African-Americans to use aesthetics to further diplomatic relations between races, Johnson was influential in inspiring this nation to finally destroy its dividing lines: "The stereotype is that the Negro is nothing more than a beggar at the gate of the nation, waiting to be thrown crumbs of civilization. Through his artistic efforts the Negro is smashing this immemorial stereotype faster than he has ever done through any other method he has been able to use. He is making it realized that he is the possessor of a wealth of natural endowments and that he has long been a generous giver to America...."

Paul Laurence Dunbar, one of the first poets to effectively employ "black dialect" as a tool in poetry, was born to former slaves in Dayton, Ohio. In school in Dayton he joined the literary society and served on the staff of the school newspaper.

In 1893, he published his first poetry collection entitled *Oak and Ivy*. His second, *Majors and Minors* (1895), was followed by the internationally recognized collection *Lyrics of Lowly Life* (1896). With an introduction by the esteemed critic **William Dean Howells**, who praised Dunbar for being "the only man of pure African blood and of American civilization to feel the Negro life aesthetically and express it lyrically...," *Lyrics of a Lowly Life* became the definitive poetic text on black experience.

Dunbar's acceptance into the literary world was one that lost him support in the African-American community. Viewed as an accommodationist more like **Booker T.**

Paul Laurence Dunbar.

Washington (see no. 24) than **W.E.B. D** **Bois** (see no. 32), Dunbar was accused o creating characters that were stereotyped b their foolish, fun-loving simplicity. He wa accused of avoiding subjects like **Jim Cro** laws and the rise in lynchings in his sho story collections, *Folks From Dixie* (1898 *In Old Plantation Days* (1903), and *Th Heart of Happy Hollow* (1904). But he wa also given credit for being one of the on poets who honestly simulated Africar American speech patterns in his wor bringing an artistic representation of blac culture to his broad national audience.

Because he was extremely popular wit white readers, Dunbar's voice was also valu able when applied to social criticism. H wrote about African-American heroes i "The Colored Soldiers" and "Harriet Beecl er Stowe," and acknowledged the pain o racism in "Sympathy," from which th phrase "I know why the caged bird sings was extracted for the title of **May Angelou**'s autobiography (see no. 89

In 1898, when the success of th industrialized North was feeding debate between blacks and white over education, Dunbar urge African-Americans to remember th rewards of classical learning. He sta ed that "People are taking it for gran ed that the Negro ought not to wor with his head. And it is so easy fo these people among whom we are liv ing to believe this." He went on t state that though men need not bur their heads permanently in scholarl works, they must temper their ne passion for industry with a passion fo art, science, and idealism. He urge them to remember the differenc between "utilitarianism and beauty."

His own artistic career was cu short when Dunbar succumbed t tuberculosis at age 33.

William Trotter, militant member of the Niagara Movement and founder of *The Boston Guardian*, was born in Chillicothe, Ohio, but raised in Boston. He went to an all-white high school before attending Harvard and gaining admittance to the prestigious Phi Beta Kappa fraternity. He graduated Harvard in 1894 and took a job in real estate after his father's example. In 1899 Trotter quit the company and opened his own, which he gave up in 1901 to found *The Boston Guardian*, which grew into the most militant African-American publication of its age.

Trotter's *Guardian* was used as a major tool against appeasement. Demanding equality without compromise, he filled its pages with attacks on the African-Americans who worked closely with white Americans to slowly alter racist policies. He was a combatant, a man willing to enter confrontations and disrupt powerful conferences in order to demand immediate and complete equality.

He was known for acts such as halting a church meeting speech by **Booker T. Washington** (see no. 24) in 1903. He spent 30 days in jail, along with fellow protester **Greenville Martin**, because he had refused to desist. He was a passionate voice against US President **Woodrow Wilson**'s segregation of Washington departments, and a man who would not join the **National Association for Advancement of Colored People**, after being very active in the preceding Niagara Movement, because he did not trust the white members of the alliance.

Along with the publication of the leftist *Guardian*, Trotter was responsible for the founding of the **National Equal Rights League**, which was supported by an entirely black membership and stood on a platform of more militant demands.

Though Trotter moved few mountains with his powerful protests and his impassioned demands, he was an important influence on the growing power of the black press in America, and a fearless voice against even the subtlest forms of racism.

In 1934, Trotter apparently leapt to his death from the roof of his Boston boardinghouse. He died a lonely man after spending much of his life in brilliant opposition to society's bias. His actions were always in answer to a growing public demand for greater civil rights.

William Trotter.

W.C. Handy, often credited with fathering popular blues music, was first told that he would be a musician by his mother; she said his big ears were the source of his musical ability. In his home town of Florence, Alabama, Handy learned to play everything from harmonicas and clay jugs to combs and broom handles.

It was in 1909 that Handy wrote his first big hit. Beginning as an election campaign song for Memphis Mayor **Edward Crump**, the famous "Memphis Blues" became a national sensation. Handy did not receive the financial benefit, but he went on to write "St. Louis Blues" in 1914, which became an even bigger hit. It was the beginning of a brand new phase in music. The blues, based on the old black spirituals, folk ballads and working man's songs, made melancholy by flatted thirds and sevenths, became one of the nation's favorite musical modes of expression.

W.C. Handy.

In his tours throughout the nation, Handy began distributing the outlawed *Chicago Defender*, published by radical civil rights activist **William Trotter**. With great risk to himself, Handy had decided to help his listeners make the move to the North away from widespread racial discrimination of the South. Some believe that when he wrote "I hate to see the evening sun go down," he referred to the danger of traveling through small Southern towns where he was not known by his face or his music, but by the color of his skin alone.

In 1918, after listening to the regional music styles of the nation, Handy began chronicling what he heard, and he and his partner, **Harry Pace**, opened the **Pace and Handy Music Company**. Along with "Beale St. Blues" in 1919, Handy went on to write a number of pieces that inspire contemporary musicians still — "A Good Man is Hard to Find" and "Careless Love" among them.

Pace and Handy flourished throughout the turbulent war years, and though Handy eventually went blind in 1943, he continued to carve a place for his music, and the music of all African-Americans. Blues music, still one of the most popular musical art forms, continues to be a credit to his innovation and that of African-American musicians around the nation.

10. ARTHUR SCHOMBURG
1874-1938

Arthur Schomburg, who's been called the Sherlock Holmes of Black History" for the extensive research that went into his collection of texts and images, was born in San Juan, Puerto Rico. It was there that he developed an intense interest in the history of fellow African-Americans. After collecting for years, he carried his wide body of historical documentation from the Virgin Islands, where he attended **St. Thomas College**, to the United States in 1891.

Schomburg worked in a law office while collecting more documents, but left the company in 1906 to join the **Bankers Trust Company**. Staying until his retirement in 1929, Schomburg continued his research while collaborating with some of the era's greatest African-American leaders.

In 1911, Schomburg and **John E. Bruce** founded the **Negro Society for Historical Research**, and in 1922, Schomburg was made president of the **American Negro Academy**, the first American group of African-American intellectuals.

Schomburg's interest in history was not just for the sake of knowledge, but for the sake of African-American identity and pride. His ideas were eloquently outlined in an essay published in 1925 entitled "The Negro Digs Up His Past," in which he stated the theories proved by history, but ignored: that the Negro has actively pursued freedom and advancement, that brilliant African-American thinkers have been treated as exceptions and the race has not been credited with their achievements, and that racially, Negroes achieved a credible, scientifically successful society without the influence of white leaders.

In order to make these assertions known, Schomburg felt that history was a tool to be used, and to be used skillfully. His collection, made up of thousands of documents and artifacts, was exceptional. In 1925, the **New York Public Library** dedicated a branch to Negro literature and history, and in 1926, over 5,000 items were bought by the **Carnegie Corporation** and donated to the branch.

When Schomburg retired, **Fisk University** made him curator of their Negro collection, until 1932, when the Carnegie Corporation made it possible for the New York Public Library to hire him as curator at the Division of Negro Literature, History and Prints, where his collection was still housed.

Schomburg continued to add to the collection, and after his death, its name was changed to the **Schomburg Center for Research in Black Culture**, where there are now over five million artifacts, photos and manuscripts, and over 100,000 books on African-American history.

Arthur Schomburg

Mary McLeod Bethune, founder of the Daytona Normal and Industrial School, was born the 15th child, but the first free child, of her family in Mayesville, South Carolina. From the beginning she was a fiercely hard worker, picking cotton, washing and ironing, and walking five miles to school each day. It was her job to bring home everything she learned and teach it to her brothers and sisters. This may have been the single most effective training Mary McLeod Bethune had in the value of education.

Mary attended **Scotia Seminary** on a scholarship, but graduated from **Moody Bible Institute** in Chicago. In 1904, she and her new husband, teacher **Albertus Bethune**, moved to Daytona, Florida and Mary began to plan the school she would one day build.

In 1904, on a piece of land used mainly for dumping, Bethune put down a five dollar payment and promised to buy the land outright for $200.00 in two years' time. She then went to work educating five little girls and her own son Albert, and by the time the bill was due on the land, Bethune had 250 students. The Daytona Normal and Industrial School, which later joined the coeducational **Cookman Institute** to form the **Bethune-Cookman College**, was firmly established.

Dedicated to education and civil rights, and specifically that of African-American women, Bethune gave a lifetime to the formation and organization of groups like the powerful **National Council of Negro Women** (1935) and the **National Youth Administration (NYA)**, which US President Franklin Roosevelt asked her to advise as the **Director of Negro Affairs**. She was also a member of the **National Association of Colored Women (NACW)**, which she aligned with the primarily whi[t] **International Council of Women**.

Working ultimately with five Unite[d] States presidents, Bethune's leadershi[p] became a respected and highly prized asse[t]. She made sure the **Women's Army Auxi[l] iary Corps** allotted 10 percent of its office[r] candidate spaces to blacks. She befriende[d] both **Franklin and Eleanor Roosevelt** an[d] was able to secure federal funding for voca[-] tional training and jobs for African-Amer[i] can youth. She secured funds for blac[k] housing projects in Florida, forced **Joh[n] Hopkins Hospital** to hire African-America[n] doctors, and appealed to Franklin Rooseve[lt] on behalf of Jewish victims during the pe[r] secution of **World War II**.

Throughout her life, Bethune worke[d] wholeheartedly for the increased power o[f] African-Americans in United States polic[y] and served those ends by offering opportu[-] nity, education and dignity.

Mary McLeod Bethune.

Garrett Morgan, inventor of many modern life savers, including the gas mask and
the three-way stoplight, was born in Paris,
Kentucky, on a farm that he left at the age
of 14. From Kentucky he headed north to
Cincinnati, Ohio, where he found work as a
handyman. He stayed in Cincinnati for six
years, working with a tutor to improve his
grammar, and moved on to Cleveland in
1895.

In Cleveland, Morgan began to focus on
the building of businesses. He took a job as
a sewing machine adjuster, but only long
enough to learn the business and open his
own sewing machine repair shop. His next
venture, a tailor shop, eventually grew to
employ 32 workers.

Through trying to improve business,
Morgan came across some of his finest

Garrett Morgan.

inventions. While trying to formulate a pol-
ish for sewing needles he discovered a way
to straighten hair. His new **Morgan Hair
Refining Company** became a huge financial
success.

It's been said that since he was the first
man in Cincinnati to own his own car, it's
possibly no surprise that he was also the
first to invent the three-way stoplight.

These inventions, though financially
rewarding, were not equal to the one he perfected in 1916, the one that saved thousands
of lives — the **gas mask**. On July 25, Morgan was summoned for what became the
most important trial run for this new invention. As 32 workers lay buried in a tunnel
below Lake Erie, where a huge explosion
had trapped them in a cell with poison gas,
Morgan, his brother **Frank**, and two volun-
teers donned the masks that had won Morgan the grand prize at the **New York Safety
and Sanitation Fair**.

Believing they had a 20 minute air supply, Morgan and his fellows went into the
tunnel, found the unconscious workers of
the **Cleveland Waterworks Company**, and

pulled them one by one to their families
and associates waiting breathlessly outside
the tunnel.

Immediately, every fire department in
the country was placing orders for Morgan's gas masks, until it was discovered that
Morgan himself was black. When orders
slowed down, Morgan hired a white man to
demonstrate the device as if he were the
inventor while Morgan assisted.

In 1917, when the United States entered
World War I, it was Morgan's improved
gas masks that protected the American soldiers from the enemy's poisonous chemical
weapons.

Though racist attitudes never managed to
defeat him, Morgan was dedicated to the
idea that African-Americans should no
longer be forced to endure them. He joined
the **NAACP**, founded the *Cleveland Call*
newspaper to improve reporting on African-
American issues, and ran for Cleveland's
City Council in 1931. Though he did not
win, he became another symbol of the growing success of African-Americans.

Carter Woodson, "the Father of Negro History" who employed scientific methods in his research of African-American roots, was born the first of nine children in New Canton, Virginia. Postponing his education so that he could help support his family, Woodson did not attend school until he was 20 years old. Self-educated, he took one year to earn a high school degree before heading to **Berea College** in Kentucky. He completed his first B.A. in 1903 and received his second, plus an M.A., from the **University of Chicago** in 1908, after taking time off to travel to Europe, Asia and Africa. Completing his Ph.D. at **Harvard** in 1912, Woodson emerged as a teacher, a historian, and a brilliant activist determined to inspire African-Americans to embrace and celebrate their own history.

Woodson's greatest achievement was the formation of a "black historiography," a body of history proven by the employment of sci-entific methods and procedures. In his man published works, including *The Education c the Negro Prior to 1861* (1915), *A Century c Negro Migration* (1918), *The History of th Negro Church* (1921) and *The African Bacl ground Outlined* (1936), Woodson detaile the history of which he was proud, an inspired his contemporaries to embrace with the same pride. Collecting historic documents and publishing them in antholc gies, Woodson brought history to life: *Negr Orators and Their Orations* (1925), *The Min of the Negro as Reflected in Letters Writte During the Crisis, 1800-1860* (1926), *Tl Miseducation of the Negro* (1933) an *African Heroes and Heroines* (1939).

He was also an active organizer. H founded the **Association for the Study c Negro Life & History** in 1915, and began t publish the *Journal of Negro History* i 1916. Interested in opening new opportun ties for education, Woodson establishe **Negro History Week**, (which ha evolved into **Black History Month**), i 1926, and began to publish the *Negr History Bulletin* in 1937, as a tool fc educators teaching black history t primary and secondary school chi dren.

Interested in factual details, an the inspirational quality of histor Woodson left many lessons for cor temporary educators and activist "We have a wonderful history behin us....It reads like the history of pec ple in an heroic age....If you read tl history of Africa, the history of yor ancestors — people of whom yo should feel proud — you will realiz that they have a history that is wortl while. They have traditions that hav value of which you can boast an upon which you can base a claim fc the right to share in the blessings c democracy...."

Carter Woodson.

Jack Johnson, the first black heavyweight champion of the world, was born in Galveston, Texas, where he attended school until the fifth grade. Leaving home soon after, Johnson took odd jobs in stables and on the docks, slowly building a reputation as a fighter. By the age of 18 he was already well-respected for "barnstorming his way through the United States," as Columbus Alley wrote.

In 1897 Johnson went professional. He married his childhood love, **Mary Austin**, and continued working toward the fight that made him an unavoidable force in the white-dominated world of professional boxing. In 1906 Johnson was granted a match with **Bob Fitzsimmons**, the former heavyweight champion of the world. In a finish that rocked the boxing world, Fitzsimmons went down and the fight ended in an unprecedented knockout. Johnson soon sought a match with the then-current champion, **James Jeffries**. Jeffries refused to fight Johnson because he was a black man and retired undefeated soon after. Jeffries' successor, **Tommy Burns**, accepted Johnson's challenge and went into the ring with him on December 26, 1908 in Australia. The world watched breathlessly as Johnson took him down too, proving himself the heavyweight champion of the world.

Known for his flashy style and his womanizing, Johnson became a thorn in the side of many white fans and fighters alike. Many wanted to see him lose badly, and when James Jeffries announced that he would come out of retirement in 1910, they thought they'd get the chance.

Jeffries made a public statement that clearly defined the racial connotations of the competition: "I fully realize what depends upon me and won't disappoint the public. That portion of the white race which is looking to me to defend its athletic supremacy may feel assured that I am fit to do my very best. I'll win as quickly as I can."

Jeffries' statement only made it sweeter when he hit the mat in the 15th round. Unfortunately, a small part of the nation couldn't accept that their champion was unequal to Johnson. Race riots erupted around the nation and both black and white citizens lost their lives before the rioters were subdued.

Johnson remained the undefeated champion until 1915, when **Jess Willard**, nicknamed "the White Hope," won the title in the 26th round of a match in Havana, Cuba.

Though there was some dispute over the knockout that ended Johnson's career, there was no question that Johnson had inspired pride in the world of African-American athletics, and paved the way for such upcoming national heroes as **Muhammad Ali** (see no. 100) and **Joe Louis**. Jack Johnson died in Raleigh, North Carolina, after receiving lethal injuries in a car racing crash.

Jack Johnson.

Oscar Micheaux was the most influential film maker to contradict Hollywood's depictions of African-Americans. He was born into a family of 13 siblings in Cairo, Illinois, and left home as a young teenager. Micheaux took a number of odd jobs before finally becoming a Pullman porter who traveled extensively throughout the nation, becoming ever more infatuated with the West. He settled a homestead in South Dakota in 1904 and founded his own publishing company so that he could release his own novels about African-American experiences in the West. His first book, *The Conquest: The Story of a Negro Pioneer*, was published in 1913 and promoted by Micheaux himself, who traveled in Western costume, selling his books directly to African-American communities. Selling them by hand, Micheaux built a national audience for each of his ten novels.

Oscar Micheaux.

When he was approached by a production company interested in adapting his novel *The Homesteader* to the screen, Micheaux demanded that he be allowed to direct it. His demands were rejected and Micheaux refused the project, but he was inspired by the idea. He founded the **Oscar Micheaux Corporation**, an independent film company in New York, and set to work in the production of non-racist representations of African-Americans in film.

Focusing on middle-class characters, African-Americans who were neither impoverished nor miserable, Micheaux cre-

ated over 35 films, including *Homestead* (1919), *Within Our Gates, The Brute, Syr bol of the Unconquered* (1920), *Son Satan* (1922), *Harlem After Midnig* (1934) and *God's Stepchildren* (1937).

Determined to counteract Hollywood stereotypical cardboard characterizations African-Americans, Micheaux focused on segment of the population engrossed in th middle-class ideals of American societ Though he is sometimes criticized for evac ing the issues of poverty and racial discrim ination, his ideal was to create a new cha acterization that did not portray Africa Americans as devoted servants or Afric savages. To these ends, Micheaux was th first to create an influential and intellige body of film that treated black America as simply Americans.

Marcus Garvey was considered a brilliant black nationalist by many — and a dangerous enemy by **W.E.B. Du Bois** (see p. 32) and other African-American intellectuals. He was born the youngest of 11 children in St. Ann's Bay, Jamaica, where he quit school early and became a printer's apprentice. In 1907, he lost his job after helping to organize a company strike. First, he moved to Costa Rica, where he worked on a banana plantation. He then went to Panama, where he worked for a newspaper, and to London, where he met **Duse Mohammed Ali** and other Africans organizing for independence. He read the inspirational works of men like **Booker T. Washington** (see no. 24) and embraced the idea that he was born to lead the black race out of degradation and poverty.

He returned to Jamaica in 1914 and founded the **Universal Negro Improvement Association & African Communities League (UNIA)**. With the desire to make the UNIA an African association that could

Marcus Garvey.

protect blacks all over the world, Garvey built a school on the model of Washington's **Tuskegee Institute**. Though it was unsuccessful, the attempt gained Garvey an invitation to visit the original university.

Coming to America in 1915, four months after Washington's death, Garvey met with civil rights leaders of the day while recruiting members for the UNIA. Though he disagreed hotly with the intellectual community headed by Du Bois, Garvey struck a chord with the rest of the American public.

By 1919, Garvey had opened branches of the UNIA in 30 cities, and had enticed over two million members. He had begun to publish *The Negro World*, which went out weekly to the West Indies, Latin America, Africa and the US. He had raised money to support the concept of an African nation led by the purest African men, and had founded the **Black Star Line**, a three-ship company with only African-American stockholders. The Black Star Line was not only a financial venture, but a way to bring African Americans back to "the African Motherland."

Garvey's popularity continued to soar as he opened the **Negro Factories Corporation**, which gave financial and technical assistance to small businesses, and in August 1920 held a month-long convention/festival in Harlem called the **First International Convention of the Negro Peoples of the World**. The delegates of the convention were so enthused that they voted to build a free republic of Africa. Garvey was to be its leader.

Before he could realize his ideal, Garvey's Black Star Line went bankrupt and he himself was tried for mail fraud. Convicted, Garvey went to jail in 1925, serving two years before US President **Calvin Coolidge** ordered him deported to Jamaica.

Garvey went to London in 1935, and lived there until a stroke took his life in 1940.

47. CLAUDE McKAY
1889-1948

Claude McKay, whose poetry is said to have ushered in the Harlem Renaissance (see no. 36), was born to farmers in Clarendon Hills, Jamaica. Leaving at the age of six to study in Montego Bay, while living with his brother who was a teacher and a minister, McKay developed a distinctive poetic style and a passion for activism.

In 1912, at the age of 25, McKay saw his first two volumes of poetry published. *Songs of Jamaica* and *Constab Ballads* were precursors to the protest poems that made McKay famous amongst the Renaissance artists. In the same year, he came to the United States to study agriculture at Tuskegee Institute under the esteemed George Washington Carver (see no. 29). He left the program within a year and took up agricultural studies at Kansas State College. He quit that program after two years and committed himself entirely to the act of writing poetry and fiction.

It was in 1919 that McKay's poetry came to stand for the sentiments of a whole new generation eager to fight continually for equality. "If We Must Die," published in *The Liberator*, punctuated the bloody summer of 1919:

If we must die—let it not be like hogs
Hunted and penned in an inglorious spot,...
Though far outnumbered, let us show us
    brave,
And for their thousand blows deal one
    death-blow!
What though before us lies the open
    grave?
Like men we'll face the murderous,
    cowardly pack,
Pressed to the wall, dying, but fighting
    back!

The volatile decade that followed brought an explosion of powerful literature, music and visual arts. The wild life of Harlem, envied by many white Americans and writ-

ten about by James Weldon Johnson (see n[] 36) and Langston Hughes (see no. 64), als[] fed the artistic life of McKay.

In 1920, *Spring in New Hampshire*, h[] next volume, was published, soon followe[] by *Harlem Shadows* (1922). His first nove[] *Home to Harlem*, was released in 1928, fo[] lowed by *Banjo: A Story Without a Pl[]* (1929), and *Banana Bottom* (1933).

A great critic of Marcus Garvey's Bac[] to-Africa movement (see no. 46), McKa[] not only used his talent to inspire and ente[] tain, but to publicly oppose what he consi[] ered a threat to African-Americans:

"The most puzzling thing about th[] 'Back-to-Africa' propaganda is the leader[] repudiation of all the fundamentals of th[] black worker's economic struggle.... A[] those who think broadly on social cond[] tions are amazed at Garvey's ignorance an[] his intolerance to modern social ideas...."

McKay traveled extensively thoug[] Europe before returning in 1934 to becom[] a US citizen, and to write his autobiogr[] phy, *A Long Way From Home* (1940). [] 1944, he converted to Roman Catholicis[] and worked among the poor in Chicago until his death in 1948.

Claude McKay.

Asa Philip Randolph, one of the nation's most successful African-American labor organizers, was born in Crescent City, Florida, where he worked for his father's tailor shop before completing high school at **Cookman Institute**. He enrolled at the **City College of New York**, and while there worked through odd jobs to note the consistent ill treatment of African-American workers.

With a prophetic drive, Randolph attempted to unionize shipyard workers during **World War I**, though he never succeeded. He co-founded the socialist paper *The Messenger* in 1917 before founding **the Brotherhood of Sleeping Car Porters & Maids** in 1925. As the first African-American trade union, the Brotherhood took some 12 years to gain recognition from the Pullman Company.

Organizing labor unions put Randolph in opposition to one of the popular leaders of his day, **Marcus Garvey** (see no. 46) and his back-to-Africa movement. Randolph said of him, "What you needed to follow Garvey was a leap of the imagination, but socialism and trade unionism called for rigorous social struggle...." However, Garvey's popularity inspired Randolph. Co-founding the **National Negro Congress** in 1936, and serving as its first president, Randolph began to organize the mass demonstrations and parades that had been so effective for Garvey. He became such a popular public figure that his persuasive promise to schedule a 100,000 person march on Washington in 1941 convinced President **Franklin Roosevelt** to issue the first ban on racial discrimination within the military. Roosevelt's order allowed a measure of equality in the armed forces, including shared quarters and shared duties, and Randolph realized how powerful mass protest could be.

In 1963, as his crowning achievement, A. Philip Randolph brought 250,000 people to Washington, D.C. to demand freedom and

A. Philip Randolph.

equality in America. After years of segregation, low wages and unequal rights, the crowd who'd come at Randolph's invitation, was treated to speakers Dr. **Martin Luther King, Jr.** (see no. 91), **Roy Wilkins** (see no. 62), **John Lewis** of the **Student Nonviolent Coordinating Committee**, and many other celebrities of the movement. His organizational skill had led to a mass gathering of people ready to accept the message of the civil rights movement. Together the nation strove for greater equality in the workforce, and a greater awareness among all Americans. As Randolph once said:

"By fighting for their rights now, American Negroes are helping to make America a moral and spiritual arsenal of democracy. Their fight against the poll tax, against lynch law, segregation, and Jim Crow, their fight for economic, political, and social equality, thus becomes part of the global war for freedom."

55

Mordecai W. Johnson, who as the president of **Howard University** pioneered programs of African-American education, was born in Paris, Tennessee, into the family of a minister at the Mt. Zion Baptist Church. He studied religion extensively, earning a B.A. from **Morehouse College** by the age of 16, a B.A. from the **University of Chicago**, a Bachelor of Divinity (B.D.) from **Rochester Theological Seminary**, a Master in Theology (M.Th.) from **Harvard**, and a Doctor of Divinity (D.D.) from both Howard University and **Gammon Theological Seminary** in 1928.

In 1926, Mordecai Johnson became the first African-American president of Howard University. He succeeded a man who had fired **Alain Locke** because Locke had wanted to make Howard a school driven by African-American culture. Johnson made it his goal to equip African-American students for higher education. He rehired Locke and invited the most esteemed African-American thinkers, including **Charles Houston** (see no. 55), **Carter Woodson** (see no. 43) and **Benjamin Mayes** (see no. 56) to teach. He doubled the size of the university's libraries and added 20 new buildings to its campus.

"The Negro people have been with us here for 300 years....Now they have come to the place where their faith can no longer feed on the bread of repression and violence. They ask for the bread of liberty, of public equality, and public responsibility. It must not be denied them."

Johnson's belief that America owed equal education, equal responsibility and equal respect to African-Americans was one that colored his entire 30-year tenure at Howard. He believed in the teaching of critical analysis, he believed in the power of Christianity, and he believed, unlike **Mar-**

Mordecai W. Johnso

cus **Garvey** (see no. 46) and his supporter that democracy was to be found in Amer ca, if each American took his place in i defense.

Under Johnson's leadership, Howar grew into one of the nation's most succes ful educational institutions for Africa Americans. His goal was to prepare his stu dents for equality and arm them with th skills of critical thinking and high thought. Programs, like Locke's envisione African Studies program, were given th freedom to grow and influence a nation ideas of education. Finally, there was anoth er well-funded, highly esteemed school o the level of the famed **Tuskegee Institu** (see no. 24) and many Howard graduate are now among the new generation's mo influential **NAACP** and civil righ activists.

Bessie Coleman, the first African-American female aviator, was born Atlanta, Texas, where he grew up promising to make something of herself. The family entertain, accountant and intellect, Bessie completed her education in a one room schoolhouse that closed during every cotton-picking season. She worked as a laundress to earn enough money to move to Langston, Oklahoma to attend the **Colored Agricultural & Normal University**. After one semester in remedial courses, her funds had run out. She returned to her mother in Waxahachie, Texas.

In 1915, Bessie moved to Chicago to live with her older brother. Employed as a manicurist on Chicago's State Street, Bessie met all the notorious figures in crime, nightclubs, gambling, and alcohol. She watched them profit as **Prohibition** transformed Chicago into a city full of danger and illegal measures.

One day, one of her brothers aimed an insult at African-American women that was meant particularly for Bessie. While talking about the French women pilots he'd served with, **John Coleman** said "You...women ain't never goin' to fly. Not like those women I saw in France." Without knowing he gave Bessie just the thing she needed to hear. "That's it," she responded. "You just called it for me."

Unable to train for a license anywhere in the United States, Bessie went to her friend **Robert Abbott** (see no. 35), publisher of **The Chicago Defender**, and enlisted his help, among others, to secure passage to Europe and tuition to the finest school in

Bessie Coleman.

France, **Ecole d'Aviation des Freres Caudron**.

Bessie returned to the United States a celebrity in 1921. Determined to attract other African-Americans to aviation, she began lecturing at schools and churches, and started giving demonstrations of her extreme skill, sometimes pulling a plane out of a nosedive mere feet from the ground. She was daring, dramatic, and considered one of the most beautiful women of the age.

Bessie was always trying to excel. Deciding to open up an aviation school, she saved up for a plane and traveled around, offering flights, performing feats and giving lectures until she could purchase it.

On April 30 she flew with a novice pilot who was helping her scout out the air field she would parachute into at the **Jacksonville Negro Welfare League**'s annual Field Day. Bessie didn't bother to buckle her seat belt, as she would have to lean out of the little **Curtiss JN4** to see where she wanted to plan her landing the next day.

Surprisingly, with pilot **William Wills** at the controls, the plane sped from 80 to 110 miles an hour, fell into a nosedive, then went into a tailspin at 1,000 feet, flipping at 500 feet, and dropping Bessie Coleman to her death. The cause was later found to be a wrench that had lodged in the control gears.

Rediscovered by contemporary aviators, Coleman is now considered an aviation pioneer, and each year, on the anniversary of her death, historian **Rufus A. Hunt** flies over her grave, dropping flowers from his plane. In addition, the **US Post Office** has finally honored Coleman and her achievements with a stamp.

Frederick McKinley Jones' inventions revolutionized the refrigeration units used on trucks, trains and airplanes so that foods and medicines could be transported safely all over the world. He was born in Cincinnati, Ohio, where he was orphaned when he was nine years old. Sent to live with a priest in Kentucky, Jones was schooled in the Catholic faith until he left for Hallock, Minnesota, in 1912. He worked fixing farm equipment while studying mechanical engineering. Returning to Minnesota after serving in **World War I**, Jones became interested in race cars and the entertainment industry. He built Hallock's first radio station transmitter, and a soundtrack system for motion pictures.

Fascinated with the challenges of machines, Jones was very interested when he overheard his boss, **Joseph A. Numero**, puzzling over the problem of refrigeration in trucks that had to transport temperature sensitive cargo. There were refrigerating devices at the time, but they were unable to withstand the movement of the trucks, and they took up valuable space.

With these concerns in mind, Jones began to experiment with new refrigerator designs. First he attached a unit to the bottom of the truck, learning quickly that mud would inevitably clog it up and destroy it. When he attached a unit to the top of a truck, Jones knew he'd found the answer.

Not only did Jones recognize the numerous possibilities, but his boss did as well. Forming the **US Thermo Control Company**, Jones and Numero began to refrigerate not only trucks, but planes, ships and trains.

Receiving over 60 patents for his inventions — 40 for refrigeration alone — Jones made it possible for the nation, and then the world, to transport fresh fruit, vegetables, dairy products and meat to any destination through refrigerated storage. His shock resistant refrigeration units led to a new frozen food industry in America.

Though Jones' inventions were originally used for commercial transportation, it soon became apparent that medicinal transportation could be life-saving. During **World War II**, it was Jones' original designs that made it possible for blood and medicine to be kept fresh for the victims of warfare. Jones was not only a creative genius, but a lifesaver of American servicemen.

Frederick McKinley Jones.

Walter White, who served a high-influential term as executive secretary for the **National Association for the Advancement of Colored People (NAACP)**, was born in Atlanta, Georgia. He attended segregated schools before entering Atlanta University and graduating in 1916. He joined a local branch of the NAACP and served as local secretary, carrying off management affairs with such dependable skill that James **Weldon Johnson** (see no. 36) befriended him, recommending him for assistant secretary of the New York office.

White took great interest in the anti-lynching campaign headed by Ida B. **Wells-Barnett** (see no. 27), and became one of the spokesmen who effectively reported on violent crime against African-Americans. Using his light complexion to help him pass as a white journalist, he

Walter F. White.

was able to infiltrate lynching areas safely and bring out the stories that were hardest to obtain.

Along with his steady, influential voice in the NAACP, White possessed a voice of great creative strength. He joined the other writers and artists of the **Harlem Renaissance** (see no. 36) with three books published between 1920 and 1926: *Rope and Faggot* (1920), *The Fire in the Flint* (1924) and *Flight* (1926).

A powerful manager and tireless activist, White, as executive secretary of the NAACP, saw the association's work begin to turn the tides of racism. He supported sharecroppers and tenant farmers in their efforts to organize, and watched the US Supreme Court rule in favor of the founding of the **Progressive Farmers Household Union of America**. The ruling, passed on *Moore v. Dempsey*, allowed farmers to

move out from under the servitude enforced by the sharecropping "accounting" system that kept them poor by design. White also supported **A. Philip Randolph** (see no. 48) when Randolph met with President **Franklin D. Roosevelt** and promised that if all military personnel weren't desegregated quickly, 100,000 people would accept his impassioned invitation to march on Washington. White was also influential in removing **W.E.B. Du Bois** (see no. 32) from his position as editor of *Crisis* and director of research and publicity. Du Bois was removed because his support for voluntary segregation violated the stated goal of the NAACP: "The Negro must, without yielding, continue the grim struggle for integration and against segregation for his own physical, moral and spiritual well-being and for that of white America and of the world at large."

53. E. FRANKLIN FRAZIER
1894-1962

E. Franklin Frazier, the great sociologist and educator, was born in Baltimore, Maryland. He graduated from Howard University in 1916 and taught at numerous schools before returning to his own education at Clark University in Massachusetts. His real passion was sociology, the behaviors of different racial groups, which he studied at Clark, and at the University of Chicago, where he earned a Ph.D. in 1931.

Beginning an illustrious career as an educator and sociologist, Frazier taught first at Morehouse College before being invited to direct Atlanta University's School of Social Work in 1922. He then taught at Fisk University from 1931 to 1934, before accepting the post as head of Howard University's Department of Sociology, which he kept until 1959.

Author Columbus Salley has said of Franklin Frazier that he was "to black soc ology what Carter Woodson (see no. 4 became to black history: the father a leading pioneer." Studying the Africa American experience sociologically, Fr zier was able to discover patterns of beha ior and to identify their positive uses: " few choice souls may rise to a moral elev tion where they can love those who oppre them. But the mass of mankind eith become accommodated to an enforced inf rior status with sentiments consonant wi their situation, or save themselves by hati the oppression and the oppressors. In t latter case, hatred is a positive moral force

By trying to understand the blac response to a society dominated by a majc ity of another race, Frazier could then spe to both about how to better unde stand one another.

To this end, Frazier publishe many books and essays that dissec ed the sociological reality of ra relations. *Traditions and Patterns Negro Family Life* was published 1934, *The Negro Family in t United States* in 1939, *The Negro the United States* in 1949, *Race a Culture Contacts in the Mode World* in 1957, the controvers *Black Bourgeoisie* in 1957 as we and the *Negro Church in Ameri* in 1962, the year of his death.

Frazier, as one of the brighte men studying racial tension, w able to take the fear away from co flict and the shame away fro African-Americans living in i often hostile environment. Frazi destigmatized African-Americi anger and made it possible to loc to the racist as well as the victim, order to understand the cause a effect of race relations.

E. Franklin Frazier.

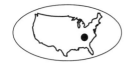

4. BESSIE SMITH
1894-1937

Bessie Smith, "Empress of the Blues," was born in Chattanooga, Tennessee, where he grew up with her six siblings. Her parents died at a very young age, so Bessie grew up under the care of her older sister Viola. Bessie grew up in harsh poverty, but she had music, and all the emotional power of a world-class performer. Retreating early into the solace of blues rhythms, Bessie started singing with her young voice on the streets for nickels and dimes when she was only nine years old.

When she was 18, Bessie obtained her first part in a show. One of her first big fans was the famous blues singer Gertrude "Ma" Rainey. Having launched a lifetime career, Smith began to travel throughout the South, singing everywhere. She could be found in clubs, theaters, anywhere people could gather.

Traveling in the South meant living daily with segregation and the threat inherent in being a new African-American woman in racist towns where she wasn't protected by her reputation as a singer. A safe place to sleep was hard to come by, as was a desegregated restaurant, or a seat on the bus.

As George Hoefer wrote, "Her blues could be funny and boisterous and gentle and angry and bleak, but underneath all of them ran the raw bitterness of being a human being who had to think twice about which toilet he could use. You cannot hear Bessie without hearing why Dr. Martin Luther King, Jr. doesn't want to wait anymore."

Even though Smith dealt with a lot of racism, she was not often afraid. Once threatened by a group of Ku Klux Klan members, Bessie chased them out, crying "You better pick up them sheets and run!"

She was a big, powerful woman who by '20 had grown into one of the nation's favorite blues singers. Crossing all race lines, Bessie drew massive crowds with her voice, and attracted some of the best musi-cians, including Charlie Green, Louis Armstrong (see no. 60) and Benny Goodman, who were honored to back her up.

She made her first record in 1923, called it "Down Hearted Blues," and watched it sell more than two million copies during a year in which Columbia Studios had even considered going out of business. Bessie herself lived like a queen, making enough money that she could be effusively generous, which hurt her later, when the Depression hit in 1929.

Bessie went back on the road, back to the harsh conditions of traveling, though poverty cut back the number of people who could afford to see her or buy her brilliant recordings. While on the road, she was critically injured in a car crash and taken to a Negro Hospital in Clarksdale, Mississippi, where she died.

Bessie Smith.

55. CHARLES H. HOUSTON
1895-1950

Charles H. Houston, an influential civil rights lawyer and the designer of **Howard University**'s Law School — which came to lead the world in the training of African-American lawyers — was born the grandson of an **Underground Railroad** "engineer" in Washington, DC. He attended the nation's first black high school, **M Street High**, and went on to **Amherst College** at the age of 15, where he was elected to Phi Beta Kappa.

Charles H. Houston.

By 1915, he was teaching English at Howard University, which he did for two years before entering into the service during **World War I**. He was made a second lieutenant field artillery officer, but was still subjected to life-threatening racism. Upon his return, Houston entered **Harvard Law School**.

After editing the *Harvard Law Review*, receiving a Ph.D. from Harvard, and doing post-doctoral work in Madrid, he was accepted into the Washington, DC Bar in 1924. He was then invited to teach at Howard University, which was already turning out 25 percent of the nation's African-American lawyers.

In 1929, Houston launched a massive program destined to turn Howard Law School into the world's finest school for African-American lawyers, "the West Point of Negro leadership." Promoting the idea that a new approach to law would help African-American lawyers influence government policy, economic freedom and social systems, Houston not only redesigned Howard's policy, but the nation's. Building a place where young

lawyers like **Thurgoo Marshall** (see no. 6 could be trained as "civ engineers," Houston beg a second program to slow ly chip away at the roo of the **Jim Crow** syster the set of laws that ma segregation and racis legal, and very difficu to rise above.

The first case w against the **University North Carolina** in 1933. was lost on a technicalit The second was fought b Marshall, who convince the **Maryland Court** Appeals to force the Un versity of Maryland to admit Donald Mu ray. Case by case, Houston and his assoc ates attacked Jim Crow laws, until the broke through.

It was Houston's tireless work that ke the "separate but equal" doctrine of *Ples v. Fergusson* from succeeding in all case The final battle, *Brown v. Board of Educ tion*, was fought by Thurgood Marsha who had followed Houston passionatel Without him, the **US Supreme Court** m not have declared segregation of publ schools illegal in 1954, four years aft Houston's death.

In 1934, Houston was asked to dire both the Joint Committee of the **NAAC** and the **American Fund for Public Servic** both of which drove passionately towa desegregation.

Houston's influence on men like Thu good Marshall was invaluable to the fig for equality, and his influence on Howa University made it possible for Africa Americans to educate themselves in tl word of law and defend themselves United States courts.

BENJAMIN E. MAYS
1895-1984

The men and women in this collection e exceptional because their lives and their complishments continue to inspire frican-Americans. **Benjamin E. Mays**, ho taught many young men, including Dr. **artin Luther King, Jr.** (see no. 91), how to rn their finest ideals into a reality, was one the men who live on as an example and educator.

Born to former slaves in Epworth, South arolina, Mays experienced the violence tween races firsthand when his father was acked by a mob in what is known as the oenix Riot of 1898. Mays was only four ars old.

He was educated in a segregated school, om which he graduated valedictorian fore attending **Bates College** in Maine, here he was elected Phi Beta Kappa.

Mays decided early after graduation to enter the ministry. He worked for his M.A. and Ph.D. from the **University of Chicago**, and served as pastor of the **Shiloh Baptist Church** in Atlanta, Georgia. Dedicated to integration and desegregation in America, Mays melded a bond between academia and the church that helped African-Americans work together to fight policies like the "separate but equal" doctrine put forth in the case of *Plessy v. Fergusson*. He said:

"We strive to desegregate and integrate America to the end that this great nation of ours...will truly become the lighthouse of freedom where none will be denied because his skin is black and none favored because his eyes are blue."

To educate all African-Americans on the value of the church in their struggle, Mays and Joseph W. Nicholson wrote *The Negro's Church* in 1930. (Mays continued his discourse in *The Negro's God*, published in 1968.)

In 1934, **Mordecai Johnson** (see no. 49) invited Mays to join **Howard University** as the dean of the School of Religion. Here, working with students like Dr. Martin Luther King, Jr., Mays' influence was invaluable in teaching modern leaders that the church could accompany them as a tool for the ideal of equality. His stirring sermons and brilliant lectures gave him a position as one of the most influential religious activists in America.

In 1940, Mays left Howard to become President of **Morehouse College**, an institution known for the quality of its graduates in the fields of medicine, law, engineering and religion. He stayed until 1967, when he was elected to the **Atlanta School Board**, over which he presided until his retirement in 1981.

Benjamin E. Mays.

Paul Robeson, the man of a million talents who applied himself to athletics, acting, and civil rights leadership, was the son of a man who had escaped slavery, and a woman who died when Paul was still a young boy. Born in Princeton, New Jersey and educated primarily in Somerville, Robeson showed an early and exceptional intellect. He was elected into the Phi Beta Kappa fraternity in his junior year at **Rutgers University** and earned 12 letters in various sports, including football. He was named All-American twice — the first African-American to win that honor. He graduated as the class valedictorian in 1919 and played professional football to work his way through **Columbia University Law School**. Completing his degree in two years, Robeson emerged from Columbia 25 years old and already turning his passion to a new career — acting.

Eugene O'Neill, one of the world's respected playwrights, saw Robeson perform and offered him the lead in his great play *All God's Chillun Got Wings* (1925). Next, Robeson was offered a role in O'Neill's famous *Emperor Jones*. Finding a new interest in music that matched his love for sports, learning, and theater, Robeson accepted composer **Jerome Kern**'s offer to play Joe in *Showboat*. With his booming, rich voice, Robeson made the song "Ol' Man River" a national favorite.

Traveling abroad, Robeson built faithful audiences all over Europe, and in 1931, accepted the role of a lifetime: "There has never been and never will be a finer rendition of this particular tragedy. It is unbelievably magnificent...." This was the sentiment repeated over and over again in the reviews for Robeson's never-to-be-equaled performance of **Shakespeare**'s *Othello*.

Mastering everything he attempted, Robeson moved on quickly. Taking up an interest in politics and race, Robeson became one of the best educated and el quent speakers of the early 20th centu Learning over 20 languages so that 1 might understand the cultures of 20 diffe ent peoples, Robeson studied differe political systems, claiming publicly that t Soviet Union was a better friend to Afric peoples than the US. He co-founded t **Council of African Affairs** in 1937, embra ing socialism because it included rac equality. He marched on Washingto protested lynching, and refused to perfo for segregated audiences.

His opinions, no matter how egalitaria brought him to the end of his career. F defense of the Soviet Union during the r scare led the US State Department to pull l passport. Unable to tour abroad, and blac listed by the entertainment industry for l socialist ideas, Robeson was unable to wo No one in the industry would hire him.

Robeson moved back to Harlem, N York and settled in. In 1958 his passp was returned. Though he tried to return his singing career, illness forbade it a Robeson lived quietly in Harlem a Philadelphia until his death.

Paul Robeson.

Duke Ellington.

Edward Kennedy Ellington, [cal]led **Duke** by fellow musicians [be]cause of his style and manners, [w]as born in Washington, DC, [w]here he was educated in segre[ga]ted schools. He dropped out of [hi]gh school as a senior and took [to] music professionally, though [he] was offered a scholarship to [Pr]att Institute in New York City [fo]r his skill as an artist. Writing [hi]s first song at 17, "The Soda [Fo]untain Rag," about the Poodle [D]og Café where he worked after [sc]hool, Ellington formed a band [ca]lled **The Washingtonians** and [to]ok it to New York City in 1922.

Though the first trip did little [m]ore than introduce the band to [in]fluential musicians like **Fats [W]aller** and **Willy Smith**, their [se]cond trip in 1923 landed a gig [at] the **Hollywood Club**. They set[tl]ed in, and within four years the [W]ashingtonians were playing the [le]gendary **Cotton Club**. After five years on [st]age and on radio shows recorded at the [C]otton Club, Ellington had gained a wide [re]putation as one of the finest composers in [A]merica. His "East St. Louis Toodle-Oo," ["M]ood Indigo," and "The Mooche" all [be]came big hits and crossed over the waters [to] a European audience.

Touring Europe, writing innovative [pie]ces like "Black, Brown and Beige," ["S]ophisticated Lady," and "The A Train," [El]lington weathered the **Depression** and [W]orld War II, appeared in films, and used [th]e "African pulse" to create compositions [th]at gained him respect throughout his life.

"The common root, of course, comes out [of] Africa. That's the pulse. The African [pu]lse. Its all the way back from what they [fir]st recognized as the old slave chants and [up] through the blues, the jazz, and up through the rock. And the avant garde. And it's all got the African pulse."

Even Ellington's voice had a rhythm and a pulse. As the musical ambassador for the US State Department, Ellington toured the Middle and Far East in the 1960s, using style and world-class rhythm to ignite respect. Prolific until his death in 1974, he conducted his own *Golden Broom and the Golden Apple* in 1965 at Lincoln Center, conducted at **Grace Cathedral** in San Francisco in 1965, and was elected to the elite **National Institute of Arts & Letters** in 1970.

His musical portfolio includes over 900 compositions, among them some of America's most exquisite. He was a welcome performer everywhere, and enchanted audiences from Chicago's **Civic Opera House** to New York City's **Metropolitan Opera House**.

65

Percy Lavon Julian, the creator of a drug that saved thousands from developing blindness, was born in Montgomery, Alabama, where his education was so poor that he had to enter remedial courses to meet his first year requirements at **DePauw University**. Determined and intelligent, Julian improved immensely, graduating as the valedictorian of his class.

Though Julian's record was excellent, and his determination to study chemistry exceptional, top rated graduate schools were still lumbering under segregationist policies. Julian taught chemistry at **Fisk University** for two years before **Harvard** accepted him as a student. After completing his graduate degree, Julian went back to teaching, working first at **West Virginia State College**, and later at the exceptional

Howard University in Washington, DC. H doctorate was completed in Vienna, whe Julian first started to experiment with t medicinal properties of soybeans.

Returning to the US, Julian used h results to create a new drug that fought t effects of glaucoma, a debilitating disea that resulted in blindness. **Physostigmi** was such a breakthrough that **Dean Bla chard** from DePauw University quickly re ommended that Julian be invited to head t university's chemistry department. Thou he'd graduated valedictorian and gone on produce an invaluable drug, racial prejudi again kept him from being offered the pos tion.

One person who was not concerned wi Julian's race was **W.J. O'Brien** of the **Gli den Paint Company**. Hiring Julian to wo as Glidden's head chemist, O'Brien foresight turned a company sufferi from heavy losses into a prospero one.

Julian opened his own pharm ceutical company in 1953. **Juli Laboratories** became an overnig success, but its creator continu researching and working toward t relief of pain and the extension life, accepting numerous awards ar an honorary Ph.D. from DePau University.

During his life, Julian develop over 100 patents, including: "**Aer Foam**," used as an extinguisher of g and oil fires during **World War II**; hormone made from soybeans th treated some forms of cancer; and system for manufacturing cortiso that was used against arthritis. Wor ing always toward the greater heal and well-being of all people, Juli produced numerous lifesaving chen ical products that furthered the evol tion of medicine.

Percy Lavon Julian.

LOUIS ARMSTRONG
1900-1971

Daniel Louis Armstrong, the innovative trumpet player known for revolutionizing jazz, was born in New Orleans, where his parents divorced when he was five. Living in a ghetto of the city where he was poorly educated, Armstrong was thrown into the Waif's Home for Boys when he fired a pistol into the air on New Year's Eve. He was 12 years old, and this unfortunate circumstance was the event that turned his life around.

While in the boys' home, Armstrong met Peter Davis, a cornet player who taught Louis how to play his first instrument. By the time he was released at age 15, Armstrong was a fine enough cornet player to become a student of Joe "King" Oliver. Oliver was a popular jazz cornetist who not only taught Armstrong the trumpet, for which he would become famous, but procured him occasional gigs with Kid Ory's band. Until 1919, Armstrong played as Oliver's backup, even taking his place when Oliver was out of town on tour. In 1922, Oliver and Armstrong paired up again in Chicago, this time playing on stage side by side. By 1924, when Armstrong took a job with the Fletcher Henderson Band in New York, jazz enthusiasts were already saying that Armstrong was the better player. By the time he returned to Chicago and organized his own band, the "Hot Five," word had spread that he was the best in America.

The "Hot Five" grew into the "Hot Seven," and songs like "Heebie Jeebies" and "West End Blues" became hits favored in America and abroad. After starring in the musical Hot Chocolates in New York, he traveled to Europe, playing for King George VI, and a crowd of over 100,000 in Ghana in 1960.

Affectionately nicknamed "Satchelmouth," and later "Satchmo," while performing at the London Palladium in 1932, Armstrong gained a notoriety, respect and familiarity amongst his fans, both for his personality and his musical definition of the black American soul.

Respected as a masterful soloist, known internationally for his manner, and nicknamed "The Ambassador of Good Will," for his effect on audiences, Armstrong continued to expand musically. His experiments brought new respect to the culture that had given the world its most soulful and celebratory sounds. Hugues Panassié, noted expert on jazz, said of him: "The whole of jazz music was transformed by Louis, overthrown by his genius. In Louis Armstrong's music is the New Orleans style at its peak, and also the basis of almost all styles that were derived from it, directly or indirectly...."

Armstrong's creative style surpassed even his instrument. Traveling throughout the world, Armstrong kept evolving, producing a new form of singing called "scat", in which simple syllables and their rhythms become the lyrics, making the voice an instrument of music that communicates through sounds instead of words.

Louis Armstrong.

67

Zora Neale Hurston, one of the celebrated writers of the **Harlem Renaissance** (see no. 36), grew up in a family of eight children in Eatonville, Florida. She lost her mother when she was nine, and was raised by her father, who later became the mayor of Eatonville. Determined to follow her mother's advise and jump at the sun, Hurston left home as a teenager and was self-supporting by the age of 14.

Working as a costumer and a maid for a **Gilbert and Sullivan** traveling show, Hurston moved to Baltimore, where she attended **Morgan Academy**, graduating in 1918. Following her passion to **Howard University**, Hurston found the mentors that could fuel her interest in the folklore and history of African-Americans. **Alain Locke** took a great interest in her work and helped her develop the style that would become famous in her short stories, novels and works of folklore.

Zora Neale Hurston.

Hurston's short story "John Redding Goes to Sea" was picked up by *Stylus* in 1921, and three years later her second story, "Drenched in Light," was published in the **National Urban League**'s *Opportunity*.

Her work was well-received, and in 1925 Hurston accepted a scholarship to attend **Barnard College** in New York, where she studied anthropology. While there, **Langston Hughes** (see no. 64), another brilliant writer of the Renaissance, collaborated with her on a magazine called *Fire!*, designed to, as Hughes said, "burn up a lot of the old, dead, conventional Negro-white ideas of the past...." Unfortunately, and ironically, their entire inventory was destroyed by fire. They teamed up again in 1930 to write the play *Mule Bone*.

Though Hurston came under the same criticism as **Paul Laurence Dunbar** (see no. 37) for presenting stereotypical images, her work has more recently been seen as a

creative body detailing the struggle of people in transition. She was a great obser er, a woman who could translate for a bro 20th century audience, black and white, t folk history that created black America.

Among Hurston's important works are t short story "Spunk" (1925), published Alain Locke's *The New Negro*, and her fol loric pieces, including *Jonah's Gourd Vi* (1934), *Mules and Men* (1935), *Tell N Horse* (1938), *Man of the Mountain* (193 her very popular novel *Their Eyes We Watching God* (1937), and her autobiograp ical work, *Dust Tracks on the Road* (1942)

She lost much of her audience in t 1940s, as protest literature became mo popular. She was falsely accused of sexua ly molesting a child, and retreated, takin jobs as a maid, a librarian, and a substitu teacher.

Hurston died in poverty but there was li tle tragedy in her life. As stated by biogr pher **Robert E. Hemenway**: "She personal believed in an integrated society, but sl spent her career trying to preserve and cel brate black cultural practices."

Roy Wilkins was executive secretary for the NAACP from 1949 to 1977, making him the leader of one of the most powerful African-American associations through the turbulent years of the civil rights movement. He was born in St. Louis, Missouri, but was raised by his aunt and uncle in St. Paul, Minnesota after his mother died of tuberculosis. Graduating from the **University of Minnesota**, where he'd edited the school newspaper and the *St. Paul Appeal*, Wilkins took a job on the *Kansas City Call*. He volunteered with the NAACP throughout his college career, but it wasn't until 1931 that Wilkins left the *Call* to join the NAACP as assistant executive secretary under **Walter White**.

Roy Wilkins.

In agreement with the established agenda of the NAACP, Wilkins supported desegregation on all levels. He was a writer who reported on the violence so prevalent against African-Americans, and he succeeded **W.E.B. Du Bois** (see no. 32) as editor of *Crisis* in 1934.

In 1949, when White took a leave of absence, Wilkins stepped in as acting secretary, and even after White's return, retained the authority to accomplish many of the daily duties of the job. In 1955, after White's death, Wilkins took up the role of executive secretary again, this time keeping the post for two decades and moving the NAACP through its delicate transition from leading civil rights organization to its new position as one among many organizations, including the militant **Black Panthers** and the **Student Nonviolent Coordinating Committee**. When young people were being arrested for sit-ins which peacefully protested the segregation of public lunch counters, Wilkins not only requested that the NAACP post bail, he submitted himself to arrest. In his own words: "We have always used persuasion through various means of political and economic pressure, but now we're going to use it much more intensely than in the past because the membership has become restless over the slow pace of the civil rights proceedings."

Wilkins was one of the chief organizers of the massive **March on Washington** in 1963. Helping **A. Philip Randolph** (see no. 48) bring 225,000 people out to hear Dr. **Martin Luther King, Jr.** (see no. 91) speak in support of civil rights, Wilkins waged one of the most successful protests in American history. He put the association's support behind the **Civil Rights Act of 1964**, and chaired the momentous **Leadership Conference on Civil Rights**.

After riots broke out into the **Watts** district of Los Angeles in 1965, Wilkins was one of the members of the **Kerner Commission**, organized to analyze the social causes. They brought this statement to the fore of the American mind: "Our nation is moving toward two societies, one black, one white — separate and unequal...." Attacking the social roots of unequal societies, Wilkins and the NAACP supported the passage of the **1965 Voting Rights Act** and the **1968 Fair Housing Act**.

Wilkins retired from the NAACP in 1977, succeeded by executive secretary **Benjamin Hooks**, who followed him in the fight for equality in America.

Marian Anderson, "the best opera singer in the world," was born in Philadelphia, Pennsylvania, where she picked up an interest in singing from her parents, who both sang in church. Marian joined the junior chorus at the **Union Baptist Church**, studied under her father, and was acknowledged as an upcoming star by the age of eight.

After singing her way through elementary school, Anderson joined the **Philadelphia Choral Society** in high school. When she was a senior, her church congregation sponsored her professional training with world-renowned voice teacher **Giuseppe Boghetti**. They worked together continually as student and mentor until Boghetti's death.

After being refused by an all-white voice school, Anderson went professional. She performed at the **Town Hall** in New York City when she was 20, but learned one of her most valuable lessons when she entered the performance ill-prepared, and sang so poorly that she considered quitting. After suffering this disappointment, she decided to work even harder, entering a competition in 1925, and winning the **Lewisohn Stadium Concert Award**. Her career had officially begun.

Anderson soloed with the **New York Philharmonic Orchestra**. She toured nationally, and then internationally. In South America, Asia and the United States, Marian Anderson played exclusively to sold out houses. Her critics began to publish statements like: "what I heard today one is priv-

Marian Anderson.

ileged to hear only i[n] hundred years." S[he] had reached a pinna[cle] of internatio[nal] appeal, but one eve[nt] in 1939 made h[er] more than a brilli[ant] contralto, it made he[r a] symbol of Africa[n] American pride.

Though Anders[on] had studied with t[he] world's greats a[nd] even played **Carne[gie] Hall**, when **Howa[rd] University** sought [to] bring her to **Consti[tu]tion Hall** in Washin[g]ton, DC, the **Daug[h]ters of the American Revolution (DA[R)]** rejected the request based on Mari[an] Anderson's race.

The protest was deafening. First La[dy] **Eleanor Roosevelt** resigned from the DA[R.] Eloquent letters, both proud and outrag[ed] hit papers all over the nation. The Secreta[ry] of the Interior, **Harold Ickes**, with the help [of] Eleanor Roosevelt, scheduled a new appea[r]ance at the **Lincoln Memorial**, and 75,0[00] people came to hear the world's best livi[ng] singer perform "The Star-Spangled Ba[n]ner," "America," and "My Soul is Anchor[ed] in the Lord." Marian Anderson found h[er]self a symbol for more than excellence. S[he] was proof that African-Americans co[uld] unite as a powerful coalition, and that wh[ite] Americans were willing to join them in t[he] fight for equality.

Marian Anderson retired in 1965, af[ter] accepting awards from the King of Swed[en] and the Emperor of Japan, after becomi[ng] the first African-American member of t[he] **Metropolitan Opera**, and after singing at t[he] inaugurations of **Dwight D. Eisenhow[er]** and **John F. Kennedy**.

4. LANGSTON HUGHES
1902-1967

Langston Hughes, called "the Poet Laureate of the Negro Race," was born in Joplin, Missouri, but raised in different cities around the Midwest and in Mexico City. He graduated high school in 1920, and in 1921 the NAACP's *Crisis* launched his career by publishing "The Negro Speaks of Rivers," one of Hughes' first poems: "I've known rivers:/I've known rivers ancient as the world and older than the flow of human blood in human veins./My soul has grown deep like rivers..."

Hughes became not only one of the first young poets to receive such honor from the NAACP, he was one of the first to signal the beginning of the Harlem Renaissance (see p. 36). One of the nation's most intense art movements, the Harlem Renaissance saw the rise of great writers like Hughes and Zora Neale Hurston (see no. 61), who later collaborated on both the publication *Fire!* and the play *Mule Bone*.

Hughes attended Columbia University for a year, but was swept up by the music and excitement of Harlem and quit. After reveling in the art and music, he left the country to travel as a sailor, writing constantly. After returning to the US, he published his first collection, *The Weary Blues*, in 1926.

Hughes' poems were immediately well received. He went back to school at Lincoln University and published his second collection, *Fine Clothes to the Jew*, in 1927. Graduating in 1929, Hughes finished his novel *Not Without Laughter*, which was published in 1930.

Traveling constantly and writing constantly, Hughes began to publish in all genres. In 1934, after spending a year in Russia, his short stories were released in the collection *The Ways of White Folks*. He covered the Spanish Civil War as a correspondent, established the Harlem Suitcase Theatre and produced his own play *Don't You Want to Be Free?*

Beginning a popular series for *The Chicago Defender* in 1934, Hughes created the character Jesse B. Semple or "Simple," who appeared in five collections, beginning with *Simple Speaks His Mind* (1950), and ending with *Simple's Uncle Sam* (1965). A year after he began writing for the *Defender*, his play *Mulatto* opened a year-long run on Broadway.

Though Hughes retains his reputation as one of the most versatile and prolific of America's writers, he is remembered primarily as a poet. *Montage of a Dream Deferred* (1951), *Selected Poems* (1963) and *Panther and the Lash* (1967) remain some of the century's finest works.

Hughes worked consistently until his death, and his works gave new respect to the African-American working class. Speaking of them in his essay "The Negro Artist and the Racial Mountain," he said: "...[J]azz is their child. They furnish a wealth of colorful, distinctive material for any artist because they still hold their own individuality in the face of American standardization."

Langston Hughes.

71

Ralph Bunche, who won the 1950 Nobel Peace Prize for his mediation during the Arab-Israeli conflict, was born in Detroit, Michigan. He moved to his grandmother's in Los Angeles, California, after losing his parents at the age of 12.

Bunche graduated from Jefferson High School in 1922, and graduated summa cum laude and Phi Beta Kappa from the University of California in 1927. With a B.A. in international relations, he entered Harvard University and graduated with an M.A. in government in 1928. Taking an immediate position in the political science department of Howard University, Bunche assisted president Mordecai Johnson (see no. 49) for a year before beginning doctoral studies at Harvard.

Continuing with postdoctoral work in the US and Britain after winning the Toppan Prize in 1934 for his dissertation, Bunche came to the attention of the Office of Strat gic Services (OSS). During World War Bunche was hired by the OSS to assist t Joint Chiefs of Staff. He was then chosen participate in the early planning sessions an important new world council, the Unit Nations (UN). Bunche was made the dir tor of the Trusteeship Division and w invited to serve on the special committee Palestine.

After World War II, there was a gr deal of highly sensitive mediation involv in partitioning Palestine in order to desi the current state of Israel. In 1948, Ral Bunche became the UN mediator in Pal tine and designed the plan to divide Pal tine into Jewish and Arab lands and pla the coveted city of Jerusalem under L supervision. The conflict between the Ara and Israelis was a delicate situation, and important one to a world not yet recover from World War II. In 1949, Bunc was able to bring about a truce, and 1950, was awarded the Nobel Pea Prize for bringing the conflict to a clo A highly-respected mediator, and a de icated civil rights activist, Bunche us his influential name to support t NAACP and other civil rights leaders the US and Africa. He also continued influence international politics throu his appointment as the UN Undersec tary for Special Political Affairs. He w instrumental in the proceedings tl brought an almost unanimous vote fr the General Assembly to denoun apartheid and call for the release political prisoners in South Africa.

Ralph Bunche resigned from the L in 1971, after having used his ent career to support the ideals of peace a justice. He died without seeing t country of South Africa dismantle system of apartheid, partly due to t American economic boycott.

Ralph Bunche.

Charles Drew, who revolutionized blood plasma research and developed the first blood banks, was born in Washington, DC, where he grew up the oldest of five children. Graduating from M Street High School — now Paul Laurence Dunbar High School — with honors in 1922, Drew entered **Amherst College**, where he became an All-American football player. Even as he developed as an athlete, he maintained that his real interest was in medicine. Following graduation, Drew took a teaching position with **Morgan College**. He focused on teaching biology, and leading the school's basketball and football teams to the championships, until he was accepted at **McGill University Medical School** in Montreal, Canada. Fascinated with the challenges of blood research — the difficulty of keeping blood fresh, and the problem of keeping all our blood types continually available — Drew began to experiment with plasma. He found that the blood's cells could be extracted, leaving the liquid intact. This liquid, or plasma, could be used in transfusions for all blood types, and kept fresh for much longer than a week, which was the average for whole blood.

Dr. Charles R. Drew.

Drew's research, beginning at McGill and continuing through the 1930s at **Howard University**, became the basis of the blood work that saved thousands of lives during **World War II**.

In 1938, Drew left Howard on leave, accepting a **Rockefeller Foundation Grant** to study at **Columbia**. As a resident in surgery at Columbia's Presbyterian Hospital, Drew took up his second field of interest, the preservation and storage of blood plasma. His excellent timing made it possible for the ideas in his doctoral thesis, entitled "Banked Blood: A Study in Blood Preservation," to revolutionize treatment of not just civilians in need of transfusions, but thousands of soldiers in the early 1940s.

Drew had returned to Howard in 1940, but left again when the **British Red Cross** invited him to treat British soldiers through the **Blood Transfusion Association**'s plasma processing program. In 1941, he returned to the US and became director of the **Red Cross Blood Bank** in New York City, where he worked to supply plasma to US soldiers.

In a famous conflict, the American Red Cross demanded that Drew not send "colored blood" to white troops overseas. If it was to be sent at all, it must be segregated. Confronting the medical ignorance of his associates, Drew announced: "Only extensive education, continued wise government, and an increasing fight on our part to disseminate the scientific facts and raise our levels of achievement can overcome this prejudice, which to a large extent is founded in ignorance." Unable to change the directive, Drew resigned from the blood program.

Drew continued to teach after the war. In 1950, he died in a car crash after falling asleep en route to a medical conference.

Born in Baltimore, Maryland, **Thurgood Marshall** became the first African-American member of the **US Supreme Court** after a career as legal counsel to the **NAACP**. Educated in segregated schools, where he was often forced to memorize passages of the **US Constitution** as punishment, and **Lincoln University**, where he received a B.A. in predentistry, Marshall chose to study law and entered **Howard University Law School**.

Thurgood Marshall.

Mentored by the brilliant designer of Howard's Law School, **Charles H. Houston** (see no. 55), Marshall was the obvious choice to succeed him as head of the NAACP's **Legal Defense Fund** in 1938. For the base of his career Marshall fought civil rights battles using the Legal Defense Fund to slowly chip away at segregationist policies.

In 1896 the Supreme Court had established a precedent by accepting the "separate but equal" interpretation that closed *Plessy v. Fergusson*. Thurgood Marshall, acting on the teaching of Charles Houston, who believed that lawyers had to work as social engineers, took the case of **Lloyd Lionel Gaines**, who was rejected by **Missouri Law School**, to the Supreme Court, winning the first case that put *Plessy v. Fergusson* into question. Arguing that no "separate" institution of "equal" value existed, Marshall convinced the Supreme Court to rule that Gaines would be admitted to Missouri University. By forcing the Supreme Court to ask the question, "What is equal?" Marshall took a step

toward the case th finally ended segreg tion in schools natio wide.

In all, Marshall too 32 cases to the Suprem Court, winning 29 them. The one that ou lawed any school segr gation was *Brown Board of Education.* 1954, he went into cou with evidence provi that separate inherent meant unequal. Sho ing through psycholog cal testing that Africa American students we disadvantaged by the removal from mainstream society, Marsha convinced the courts to overthrow *Ples v. Fergusson*, a dangerous stumbling blo for African-Americans seeking equali Though it took many court battles to pro it, there was no longer a legal leg to sta on in favor of segregation.

Winning against the Board of Educati was not Marshall's only goal. He coordin ed legal battles against discrimination voting and housing. He was not only t main legal counsel for the NAACP, but w appointed by **John F. Kennedy** to the **U Court of Appeals** in 1961. None of his de sions were overturned by higher courts. I was appointed US solicitor general by Ly don B. Johnson in 1965, and Johns appointed him to the US Supreme Court 1967, where he became a national symb for the rights and freedoms of disadva taged Americans.

After serving as one of the most respe ed members of the court, Marshall retired 1991, replaced by **Clarence Thomas**, t second African-American man to serve the nation's highest court.

58. ADAM CLAYTON POWELL, JR.
1908-1972

Rev. **Adam Clayton Powell, Jr.**, chairman of the **House Education and Labor Committee** from 1961 to 1967, was born in New Haven, Connecticut, but raised in Harlem, where his father was the minister of **Abyssinian Baptist Church**. He was educated at **City College of New York** for two years, and at **Colgate University**, from which he graduated with honors. Expecting to go on to **Harvard Medical School**, Powell was surprised to receive a call to the ministry. Hearing a voice ask who would succeed his father as minister of the biggest church in Harlem, Powell changed his direction and entered **Teacher's College of Columbia University**.

In 1938, when he was 30 years old, Rev. Powell succeeded his father and began to use the church as a tool for social engineering. Gathering support for boycotts of businesses that wouldn't hire African-Americans, Powell founded the **Coordinating Committee for Employment**. The committee coined the famous phrase, "Don't buy where you can't work," helping the African-American community to think of itself as an economic block that could wield power with its choices in the marketplace.

In 1941, after he'd proved himself a brilliant organizer, Powell was elected to the **City Council** of New York. In 1944, with the support of such powerful men as **A. Philip Randolph** (see no. 48), Powell was named Harlem's first African-American congressman.

He was elected to chair the powerful **House Education and Labor Committee** in 1961, and helped pass the **Civil Rights Act** in 1964, the **Economic Opportunity Act** in the same year, and the **Voting Rights Act** in 1965. Praised by

President **Lyndon B. Johnson** for passing the **Anti-Poverty Act**, the **Minimum Wage Act**, the **Vocational Education Act** and the **National Defense Education Act**, chairman Powell was shocked when, in 1967, he was expelled from the **House of Representatives**. Founded on dubious accusations of "misuse of funds," his dismissal was a shock that went through the whole nation, ending in massive protests.

In 1967, he was reelected to his seat by his loyal supporters in Harlem, and took his case to the courts. In 1969, Congress reversed its decision. Powell was returned to his seat, fined $25,000 and stripped of his position. The courts upheld that Congress had acted outside its jurisdiction.

Powell was defeated in 1970, and died in 1972, described by **Gil Noble** as "...a fighter. If he did play, he worked harder than he played. Most of all, he was a fighter."

Adam Clayton
Powell, Jr.

Richard Wright, born in Roxie, Mississippi, was raised in a family that suffered constantly from poverty. When Wright's father deserted the family in 1913, Richard's mother moved them to Tennessee and then Arkansas, until she became ill, and put him and his little brother into an orphanage. Rescued by his maternal grandparents, who brought the boys to Jackson, Mississippi, Richard began to attend school regularly for the first time. His mother had taught him to read and he had decided early that he would be a writer, but the racism in Mississippi was so extreme that no opportunity would have presented itself. In desperation, Wright pulled off a small robbery and used the money from the sale of a gun and some fruit preserves to buy a ticket to Memphis.

In 1927, he moved to Chicago and started writing for *Left Front* and *New Masses*. When the **Depression** struck, Wright was chosen for government writing projects that kept him employed and further increased his skill. In 1935, Wright chose the **Joe Louis/Max Baer fight** as the subject of a short piece defining "the heart of the Negro:" "Here's the fluid something that's like iron. Here's the real dynamite that Joe Louis uncovered."

In 1937, Wright moved to New York, and in 1938 his first collection of stories, *Uncle Tom's Children*, appeared. Built on his experiences with intense and violent racism in the Deep South, these stories defined the strength of the African-American character trying to succeed against all odds. Well received, *Uncle Tom's Children* was followed by Wright's first — and most famous — novel, *Native Son*, which follows the character **Bigger Thomas** through the trials of being black in the North, held down in a "cold and distant world; a world of white secrets carefully guarded."

Richard Wright.

Twelve Million Black Voices, Wright folk history, was published, quickly fo lowed by *Black Boy* in 1945, which to Wright's own story of growing up in the ru al South. Though there are questions as to i authenticity as an autobiography, the funda mental truth of *Black Boy* gained it a fo lowing as respectful as that of *Native Son*.

Wright left America for Paris in 194 where he continued to write amongst group of other intellectuals, artists and wri ers including **Gertrude Stein, Jean Pau Sartre** and **Simone de Beauvoir**. *The Ou sider* was published in 1953, *Savage Hol day* in 1954, *The Long Dream* in 1959 an *Eight Men* in 1961.

After Wright's death in Paris, **Jam Baldwin** (see no. 85) observed: "Wright unrelentingly bleak landscape was not mer ly that of the Deep South, or of Chicago, b that of the world, of the human heart."

Katherine Dunham, one of the nation's most influential choreographers, and a devoted activist for all people of African heritage, was born in Glen Ellyn, Illinois. She lost her mother when she was only three, and she and her brother were moved to South Chicago, where they stayed with an aunt while their father traveled as a salesman. Their father regained custody when Katherine was five, and the reunited family, with the addition of Annette Poindexter, Katherine's new stepmother, moved to Joliet, Illinois.

Always active, Katherine took private piano and dance lessons from elementary school on, applying her agility and grace to athletics when she reached high school. She was elected president of the Girls' Athletic Association before attending Joliet Township Junior College, and later, University of Chicago. There Katherine began to study cultural anthropology with a passion. Pursuing her education in ethnology and African cultures, she began to mix historical tradition with her creative approach to dance. Form-

ing Ballet Negre with dancers Ruth Page and Mark Turbyfill, Katherine launched a career as one of the finest choreographers in America. Negro Rhapsody, their debut performance at the Beaux Arts Ball in 1931, established Katherine as an expert on African dance styles, and she was chosen in 1933 to handpick 150 young dancers to perform a piece of her own design at the Chicago Century of Progress Exposition.

Dunham's work was filling a void in American dance that had never been explored before. Granted the Rosenwald Travel Fellowship in 1935, she went to Jamaica, Martinique, and Haiti to further study the origins of the Caribbean styles that formed the basis of her own original pieces.

She graduated from the University of Chicago in 1936 with a degree in anthropology, and moved to Northwestern University, where she completed her doctorate under Melville Herskovitz, an anthropology expert who was also one of the first essayists of the Harlem Renaissance (see no. 36).

Dunham's Ballet Negre grew into the Negro Dance Group and toured over 60 countries, bringing traditional African ritual to different nationalities in the form of Caribbean-inspired dance. Her choreographed pieces include Ballet Fedre (1938), Tropics and Le Jazz Hot (1940), Tropical Review (1943), Bal Negre (1946), Caribbean Rhapsody (1950), and Bamboche (1962). Documenting the history of African descended cultures, Dunham wrote Journey to Accompong (1946), Les Danses d'Haiti (1950), and A Touch of Innocence (1959).

After retiring from the stage in the 1960s, Dunham founded the Katherine Dunham Center, where she trains young people in African dance and culture. Always a supporter of African-inspired cultures, Dunham went on a hunger strike in 1992 in support of fleeing Haitians who weren't granted asylum by the Bush Administration.

Katherine Dunham.

71. BAYARD RUSTIN
1910-1987

Bayard Rustin, the brilliant aide to A. Philip Randolph (see no. 48) and Dr. Martin Luther King, Jr. (see no. 91), added the Gandhian ideal of pacifism to the modern civil rights movement. He was born in West Chester, Pennsylvania, where he suffered at the hands of his peers. Inventing his own flamboyant character by impersonating his stepfather's Indian accent and enduring the early bullying he took from schoolmates for his extreme intelligence, Rustin sought true community in Cheyney State College and Wilberforce University in Ohio.

Attracted to socialism but disillusioned when the socialists avoided issues of racism, Rustin joined the Young Communist League in 1936. Performing in Harlem as a musician, and recruiting for the Young Communist League, Rustin found a society he could charm and influence. He left the League in 1941 to join Fellowship for Reconciliation, which grew into the influential Congress of Racial Equality (CORE).

President A. Philip Randolph had been quick to spot Rustin's unique ability to organize and endure enormous pressure in order to maintain a movement. Rustin joined Randolph as his assistant, and helped organize the threatened march on Washington, DC, that convinced President Franklin D. Roosevelt to end discrimination in the military.

Always looking for the next project, Rustin was one of the first to get involved in the freedom rides. Rustin tested the new US Supreme Court ruling that African-Americans didn't have to sit at the back of the bus by riding in the front of an interstate bus through the South with other members of CORE. They were arrested and Rustin and his associates served 22 days in jail when the NAACP could not legally defend them because of lost evidence. Rustin was the first to view the punishment as a possible way to teach peace through lack of resistance.

Leaving CORE, Rustin became an ai␣ to Dr. Martin Luther King, Jr. when he a␣ 150 others were held legally responsible f␣ the Montgomery bus boycott. Helping Ki␣ face arrest without resistance, drafting t␣ original plan for the Southern Christi␣ Leadership Conference and assisting ␣ Philip Randolph in the organization of t␣ massive, 1963 March on Washingto␣ which became the symbol for not just t␣ civil rights movement, but all moves for li␣ erty and equality in the US, Rustin was ␣ invaluable and brilliant activist.

Until his death, Rustin headed the ␣ Philip Randolph Institute in New Yo␣ where he never surrendered his belief ␣ nonviolence and complete, uncompr␣ mised equality.

Bayard Rustin.

ROSA PARKS
1913-2005

Rosa Parks is known for touching off the Montgomery bus boycott in 1955 that led to the extreme popularity of Dr. Martin Luther King, Jr. (see no. 91) and the modern civil rights movement. She was born Rosa McCauley in Tuskegee, Alabama, and attended school throughout the state, living with relatives until her mother's failing health begged her return. In 1932, she married Raymond Parks and worked numerous odd jobs, joining the NAACP in the early 40s and acting as youth advisor and secretary for the Montgomery Chapter. She later joined State President **Edgar Nixon** and served as his office manager.

In December of 1955, when Rosa Parks, then a seamstress at a department store, refused to yield her seat on the bus to a white man as dictated by law. She was not the first woman to refuse to rise, but she was the first of impeccable reputation and upbringing. While Rosa Parks was jailed on December 1, 1955, Edward Nixon's friend **Ann Robinson** was up all night with other members of the **Women's Political Council**, making the first flyers that announced a one day boycott of the Montgomery bus line on December 5, the day Rosa Parks was going to trial after being released on bail. Since 75 percent of bus riders were African-Americans, the financial repercussions were definitely damaging.

Robinson told Nixon of the plan while the flyers went up in African-American communities. When he told the NAACP that Rosa Parks, the mild, polite, well-dressed young secretary in Montgomery

Rosa Parks.

was arrested for refusing to forfeit her seat, they gathered together at Dr. Martin Luther King, Jr.'s **Dexter Baptist Church** and decided that this would be the case they'd fight all the way to the **US Supreme Court**. The **Montgomery Improvement Association**, headed by Dr. Martin Luther King, Jr., not only approved the boycott, but ensured that it lasted for 381 days, nearly crippling the bus line.

On December 5, Rosa Parks lost her court case, but won the support of Montgomery's African-American populace. As bus after bus ran through town without any black passengers, Parks' case was appealed. Finally, on December 20, 1956, the Supreme Court upheld the **United States District Court** ruling that segregation on public buses was unconstitutional.

Rosa Parks had begun what has been called the most important American movement since **Emancipation**, but she was far from retiring. In 1957, Parks moved to Detroit, Michigan and worked with the **Southern Christian Leadership Conference**, which annually sponsors the **Rosa Parks Freedom Award**. From 1957 to 1988, she assisted US Representative **John Conyers**, and in 1980 received the Dr. **Martin Luther King, Jr. Nonviolent Peace Prize**. In 1987, she established the **Rosa and Raymond Parks Institute for Self-Development**, which assists teenagers, and in 1990, was joined by 3,000 government and community leaders in honor of her 75th birthday at the **Kennedy Center** in Washington, DC.

Jesse Owens, who took four gold medals in the 1936 Olympics, was born James C. Cleveland in Danville, Alabama, the seventh of eleven children. His family was very poor and James Cleveland, or J.C. as he was called, went to work at the age of seven picking cotton. His family moved to Cleveland, Ohio, and J.C. joined the Fairmont Junior High School track and field team. At East Technical High School, a teacher mispronounced his initials, and J.C. became Jesse for good.

Owens began running track in high school and continued while at Ohio State. In May, 1935, he competed in the Big Ten College Track and Field Championships and broke three world records. He qualified for the 1936 Olympic Games.

Owens competed at the Games in Berlin, Germany, where Adolf Hitler watched him challenge and defeat Germany's Aryan ath-

letes. Owens took four gold medals, deli ering a stinging blow to Hitler's theory Aryan superiority. In the hundred met two hundred meter, long jump and fo hundred meter relay, Owens beat t world's top athletes — of all races.

Though a story circulated that Hitl snubbed Owens at the presentation cerem ny, Owens denied the rumor, though admitted that Hitler watched him with b terness. As writer Columbus Salley point out, "Owens and his athletic records lo outlived Adolf Hitler and the Third Reich

When Owens returned home to the U he was met by a ticker tape parade. Held as a national hero, he was particular embraced by African-American athlete who used his example to help them bre through stereotypes everywhere.

Owens, though one of the world's great athletes, did not have a job to support h wife and two children. Accepting position as a playground instruct because he couldn't afford to fini college, Owens worked for $30 a we until he was offered a huge prize if could beat a racehorse in the hundr yard dash. The prize money w enough to send Owens back to colleg where he completed his degree. joined other ventures, including a cha of dry cleaners, but when his busine partner disappeared, leaving Owe thousands of dollars in debt, he took job with the Ford Motor Company.

The Owens family moved Chicago in 1949, where Owens w able to use his reputation as a to Going into public relations, Owe began lecturing on athletic superiori as a tool for building teams betwe races. He was granted the Medal Freedom by US President Gerald Fo in 1976, four years before he died lung cancer.

Jesse Owens.

KENNETH B. CLARK
1914-2005

Kenneth Clark, who developed the psychological arguments that won the influential *Brown v. Board of Education* (see no. 67) case, was born in the Panama Canal Zone where his father worked. In 1919, Kenneth and his mother returned to Harlem in New York City by themselves. Kenneth went to integrated schools and studied under inspirational mentors like **Countee Cullen**, who was a teacher at **Junior High School 139**, and **Arthur Schomburg** (see no. 40),

Kenneth Clark.

who was available as the curator of the **New York Public Library**'s Division of Negro Literature, History & Prints.

Clark went from **George Washington High School** to **Howard University** and to **Columbia**, where he earned a Ph.D. in psychology. Teaching at **City College of New York** from 1942 on, Clark began writing about the psychological effects of segregation. Working from the theories and explanations laid down by **E. Franklin Frazier** (see no. 53), Clark developed proof that segregated African-American children began at a disadvantage simply because they'd been excluded as a group.

In 1953, Clark published both *Desegregation: An Appraisal of the Evidence* and *Prejudice and Your Child*. In 1954, **Thurgood Marshall** (see no. 67) used Clark's research to sway the court in the famous *Brown v. Board of Education* case that found segregation unconstitutional. He used examples like the experiment in which African-American children were invited to choose from a collection of white, Japanese and black dolls. In each instance, the chil-

dren preferred the black dolls least. From these results, Marshall was able to illustrate that even from a very young age, African-American children recognized that their segregation from white children was based on a judgement made against them. When the justices of the **US Supreme Court** agreed that the evidence was sound, they could no longer accept the "separate but equal" argument of *Plessy v. Fergusson*.

Throughout the 1960s, Clarke added his research and analysis to the debate raging between the pacifist African-American organizers following Dr. **Martin Luther King, Jr.** (see no. 91) and the more militant followers of **Malcolm X** (see no. 87).

Following E. Franklin Frazier in asserting that "The natural reactions to injustice, oppression, and humiliation are bitterness and resentment," Clark defended militancy as a healthy response.

Clark's ideas, when applied to a historical context, ring true in a painful way: "I read that report...of the **1919 riot in Chicago**, and it is as if I were reading the report of the investigating committee on the **Harlem riot of '35**, the report of the investigating committee on the **Harlem riot of '43**, the report of the **McCone Commission** on the **Watts riot**..."

After the **Los Angeles riots** of 1992, perhaps it is even more important to recognize Clarke's assertion that racism must constantly be fought because "injustice, oppression and humiliation" are often followed by acts of "bitterness and resentment."

75. BILLIE HOLIDAY
1915-1959

Billie Holiday, born **Eleonora Fagan** in Baltimore, Maryland, was easily one of the most beguiling singers of the 1930s, 40s and 50s. She started singing publicly in **Jerry Preston's Log Cabin Club** at the age of 15, but people remember her voice from long before that. Singing at the **Hot-Cha Bar and Grill** in Harlem, Billie was heard by **Ralph Cooper**, who reported her talent to **Frank Schiffman**, owner of the **Apollo**. Getting her first gig at the Apollo in 1934, backed up by **Bobby Henderson** on piano, "**Lady Day**," who had already appeared in **Paul Robeson**'s film *The Emperor Jones* (see no. 57) and a short film with **Duke Ellington** (see no. 58), "tore the house down." Already living fast and hard, Billie sang with **Count Basie**, **Artie Shaw**, and everyone else known for making music in the 1930s.

By the 1940s Billie was famous in her own right, singing solo all over the country. She was named *Esquire*'s top female vocalist in 1944 and 1945, and had recorded with **Benny Goodman**, Basie, Shaw and **Eddie Heywood**. Her recordings of "Lover Man" and "Strange Fruit" sold over a million copies, and her recordings of hits "Gloomy Sunday," "I Cover the Waterfront," "Am I Blue?" and a hundred others are still considered major influences in the careers of contemporary stars.

Frank Sinatra said of her performances in the famous 52nd Street clubs in New York City: "With few exceptions, every major pop singer in the US during her generation has been touched in some way by her genius. It is Billie Holiday who was, and still remains, the greatest single musical influence on me."

Billie Holliday

Currently available retrospective groupings of her work include *Billie Holiday* (1959), the *Golden Years*, two volumes of collected material from 1933-1942 (1962), *Lady Day*, collected work from 1935-1939 that appeared in the mid-1950s, and *Lady in Satin* (1958).

Though Billie's success as a singer was magical, her life was a constant struggle. Battling with drug addiction and a passion for hard living, Billie relied heavily on her friends and fellow musicians to support her. Her autobiography, *The Lady Sings the Blues* (1956), was written with journalist **William Dufty**, and the movie of the same name, starring **Diana Ross**, was released in 1972.

82

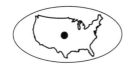

Gwendolyn Brooks, the 1949 Pulitzer rize winning poet, was born in Topeka, ansas, but moved to the south side of hicago when she was a month old. Her lent with words was marked at a very ear- age. By the age of seven, she could fill a ige with verse. By the age of 13, these erses were good enough for publication. Eventide" was published in *American hildhood* magazine in 1930, and when ie entered high school a year later, teach- 's like **Langston Hughes** (see no. 64) and imes **Weldon Johnson** (see no. 36) were vailable to inspire and encourage her ork. She graduated from **Englewood igh School** in 1934 — the same year in hich *The Chicago Defender* egan to publish her poems eekly — and **Wilson Junior ollege** in 1936.

Brooks' work won immediate cognition. The **Midwestern /riter's Conference** awarded rizes to her each year from 1943 1946. Her first volume of poet- ;, *A Street in Bronzeville* 945), made her one of *Made- oiselle* magazine's "10 women the year," and a **Guggenheim ellowship**, awarded in 1946, iade it possible for her to con- entrate on writing her second olume of poetry, *Annie Allen*, hich won her the 1949 Pulitzer rize for poetry.

It has been said of Brooks' ork that her first volumes are :quisitely constructed poems ill of craft, but only lightly igaged with the emotional lives f individuals. Later works, cluding *The Bean Eaters* 960), *Selected Poems* (1963) id *In the Mecca* (1968), are said / **Norris B. Clark** to show a

dawning awareness of the social concerns of African-Americans. The next phase of her career, yielding *Riot* (1969), *Family Pictures* (1970), *Aloneness* (1971), and *Beckonings* (1975), he says are "less devoted to craft and more concerned about pronounced statements on a black mystique, the necessity of riot (violence), and black unity."

Continuing to evolve as an artist, and also as a social critic, Brooks added *Primer for Blacks* in 1980, *Mayor Harold Washington and Chicago, The I Will City* in 1983, *The Near-Johannesburg Boys and Other Poems* in 1986, *Blacks* in 1987, and *Winnie* in 1988.

Gwendolyn Brooks.

Ossie Davis and Ruby Dee, who built what W. Calvin Anderson called a "sober allegiance to a proud African oral tradition and a rich African-American folklore," met for the first time through the Rose McClendon Players, a New York theater troupe. In 1947, after performing together in *Jeb Turner*, they were married. Still performing together — *Do the Right Thing* (1989), and *Jungle Fever* (1991) — Davis and Dee remain important role models for anyone interested in the artistic representation of African-American culture.

Ossie Davis was born in Cogdell, Georgia, and educated in segregated schools, later attending Howard University, where he studied under Alain Locke. He quit Howard to pursue a career as an actor and writer in New York City, but was drafted a year later, in 1942, and forced to leave the Rose McClendon Players for a term as a surgical technician in Liberia.

Ruby Dee joined the Rose McClendon Players while Davis was in the service. She had come from Harlem with a B.A. from Hunter College in 1945.

After apprenticing with the America Negro Theatre, she began to work with the Rose McClendon Players, where she m Davis on his return from Africa.

Together, they became one of the nation's key entertainment teams. They co laborated on the film *No Way Out* in 195 the play *Alice in Wonder* in 1952, the pl *Purlie Victorious* in 1961, the film versio called *Gone Are the Days* in 1963, the nin part television series *The History of Neg People* in 1965, a record called *The Poet of Langston Hughes* in 1964 and their ow television series called *The Ruby Dee/Oss Davis Story Hour* in 1974.

Though interested in bringing the broa scope of African-American experience all Americans through the act of stor telling in modern media, Dee and Dav were also committed activists. Associate with the NAACP, the Student Nonviole Coordinating Committee, Dr. Mart Luther King, Jr.'s Southern Christian Lea ership Conference, and the Congress Racial Equality, Davis and Dee have bee tireless promoters of African-Americ pride. Ossie Davis was the M.C. for t 1963 March on Washingto and Dee established t Ruby Dee Scholarsh in Dramatic Arts.

Ruby Dee and
Ossie Davis.

FANNIE LOU HAMER
1917-1977

Fannie Lou Hamer, a woman who nearly lost her life while trying to register African-American voters in the Deep South, was born a sharecropper in a family of 20 in Ruleville, Mississippi. In sharecropping, the land was leased from a white landowner. The family would live and work the land and split the crop with the landlord. Often all expenses, including fertilizer and seed, came from the sharecropper's share. Because the work was so hard, constant, and exhausting, children like Fannie had to leave school at a very early age to help support the family. She was picking cotton at the age of six, and working full-time cutting cornstalks by early adolescence.

In 1944, Fannie left her family's farm and moved in with her husband, **Perry Hamer**. He too was a sharecropper, and Fannie worked with him, rising to a relative position of prominence as the plantation timekeeper.

In the early 1960s, when the South was still resistant to the growing **civil rights movement**, the **Southern Christian Leadership Conference (SCLC)** and the **Student Nonviolent Coordinating Committee (SNCC)** traveled through the South, encouraging African-Americans to take the dangerous steps towards claiming their right to vote. Fannie Lou Hamer decided to register. She was fired from her job the day after she did. After 18 years on the plantation with her husband, Hamer was told by her landlord that pressure from the **Ku Klux Klan** would be so excessive that she had to leave. Hamer fled that night. The house where she and other registered voters stayed was sprayed with bullets soon after.

With a new commitment, Hamer joined other brave people in organizing a voter registration drive that not only covered Mississippi, but grew into the **Mississippi Freedom Democratic Party (MFDP)**. Enduring a vicious beating during a four-

Fannie Lou Hamer.

day detainment in Greenwood, Mississippi, Hamer learned firsthand how powerful and frightening her actions must be. After detaining her and fellow activists, police officers ordered other black prisoners to beat her with a blackjack until they were too tired to continue. Neither Hamer nor her fellow protesters gave up. If they had, men like Dr. **Martin Luther King, Jr.** (see no. 91) might not have been able to gain the support of African-Americans in the Deep South.

Adding to a movement that touched not just Mississippi's politics, but the politics of the nation's new generation, Hamer forced Mississippi's all-white delegation at the **Democratic Convention** in 1964 to respond to the accusation that it adhered to traditions that deliberately and consistently excluded African-Americans. This kind of pressure, steady and determined, was invaluable to the guarantee of voting rights for all Americans.

85

John H. Johnson, publisher of *Ebony* and *Jet* magazines, was born in Arkansas City, Arkansas. John lost his father when he was six, and grew up an only son with his mother and his stepfather. In Chicago, where his family moved in 1933, John graduated from **Jean Baptiste Pointe De Sable High School** and attended the **University of Chicago** while working part time at Supreme Life Insurance Company. He then attended **Northwestern University School of Commerce.** Supreme Life made him editor of its in-house journal, *The Guardian,* which inspired him to formulate and publish his first piece, the *Negro Digest* (1942).

A traditional African-American paper "dedicated to the development of interracial understanding and the promotion of national unity," the *Negro Digest* taught Johnson that there was a black consumer community that had not been addressed by white-owned companies. Changing his style, Johnson began to publish the stylish *Ebony* in 1945, coaxing businesses to turn to the African-American community as a consumer market. Though white-owned businesses may have been the first to profit, soon African-American readers were inspired to open their own businesses to fulfill the needs of African-Americans, who were quickly becoming more vocal in the marketplace.

Johnson continued to build on his investment. In 1950, he published the first issue of *Tan,* and in 1951, *Jet.* Finding glamour an irresistible allure, Johnson developed his own cosmetic line, **Fashion Fair Cosmetics**, which was tied to the annual, and international, *Ebony* Fashion Show. By the late 1980s Johnson had become a million aire many times over, and his conglomerate business was employing nearly 2,000 people in the fashion, radio, print and cosmetics industries.

Not only did Johnson's enterprises add an African-American voice to America's economic debates, but they added a sense of self to Americans who had previously been ignored. Coerced, seduced, lured toward an elegant lifestyle by images of successful African-Americans, readers began to shift their self-perception, seeing themselves reflected in the American dream in a new way — black and beautiful.

John H. Johnson.

Jack Roosevelt Robinson, the first African-American baseball player to see his team to the **World Series**, was born in Cairo, Georgia. His family lived there for a year before his father deserted them and Jackie's mother moved them to Pasadena, California. Jackie attended **Pasadena Junior College** before transferring to the **University of California at Los Angeles**, where he was the first student to gain letters in baseball, basketball, football and track. In his third year, Robinson quit school and played for the **Los Angeles Bulldogs** before being drafted into the army in 1942.

Robinson applied for the **Officers' Candidate School (OCS)** and was turned down because of his race. Aggravated and insistent, Robinson complained to the highest level. Heavyweight champion **Joe Louis**, who was also stationed at Fort Riley, Kansas, used his connections to have Robinson admitted. He became a second lieutenant, later admitting how difficult it was: "I was naive about the elaborate lengths to which racists in the armed forces would go to put a vocal black man in his place."

In 1944, Robinson finally returned to his career as a baseball player in the US. Joining the **Kansas City Monarchs**, an all black team playing in an all black league, Robinson came to the attention of the **Brooklyn Dodgers'** president and general manager **Branch Rickey**, who had sent scouts out into the **Negro League** after deciding to be the first team to desegregate baseball.

Robinson met Rickey in 1945 and promised that he could take any pressure that came from his being the first African-American ball player in the white league. Already aware how extensive racism can be, Robinson was prepared when his presence nearly led to a strike.

Robinson's team members signed a petition for his removal, the president of the **Philadelphia Phillies** refused to play against the Dodgers while Robinson was on the roster and the **St. Louis Cardinals** sent out word that they would strike.

In response, the president of the **National League** was forced to make a statement. Coming down on the side of integration, he said to the Phillies, "If you do this, you will be suspended from the league....I don't care if it wrecks the National League for five years. This is the United States of America, and one citizen has as much right to play as another."

Though the first years were tough, and Robinson had to be twice as good as his best competitors to be accepted, in 1947 he became the first African-American ball player in the World Series and was named **Rookie of the Year**. In 1949 he won the **Most Valuable Player** Award.

He retired in 1958, after a year with the **San Francisco Giants**, and died knowing that the world of sports was now open to players of all races.

Jackie Robinson.

87

81. DANIEL "CHAPPIE" JAMES, JR.
1920-1978

Daniel James, Jr. was the seventeenth child of a family in Pensacola, Florida. His mother managed a school for African-American children and taught her own children and others the value of leadership and a strong will. In 1937, James, nicknamed "Chappie," entered Booker T. Washington's Tuskegee Institute (see no. 24) in Alabama. Though he was a popular, promising young man, he was expelled from the university two months before graduation because he was caught fighting with another student.

Deciding to join the army after having learned to fly an airplane at Tuskegee, James applied to a **US Army Air Corps** advanced flying program, also at Tuskegee. In 1943, as a second lieutenant, he was assigned to the **477th Bombardment Group** at Selfridge Field near Detroit. Racism was still prevalent in the armed forces, and African-American officers were rarely promoted or allowed into officers' clubs and facilities, despite a regulation making segregation in these clubs illegal.

The 477th was transferred to Indiana after incidents of racial tension grew too heated. When the officers realized that racism was as rampant in Indiana, they staged a peaceful sit-in at a segregated officers' club. The protesters were arrested and charged with mutiny. When James and over 100 other officers came out in support of them, they too were arrested. Among the bold officers who risked their careers were **Coleman Young**, later elected mayor of Detroit, and the future secretary of transportation under President **Gerald Ford**, **William T. Coleman**.

In 1948, years after the officers were released by General **George C. Marshall**, President **Harry S. Truman** issued Order 9981, making segregation in the armed forces illegal.

James had begun a distinguished career. He was in the Philippines, where he was

Daniel James, Jr.

injured while saving the life of a fellow pilot. He flew 101 missions in Korea and was awarded the **Distinguished Flying Cross**. He was made Deputy Commander for Operations for the US Air Force's 81st Fighter Wing at Bentwaters, England, and later as a vice wing commander in Vietnam where he flew 78 missions.

Confident and highly skilled as a leader, James faced Colonel **Muammar Qadhafi**, leader of Libya, in a confrontation in which Qadhafi rolled armored vehicles through **Wheelus Air Force Base** in 1969, demanding the US abandon the lease that granted them the base until 1970. Qadhafi himself met James with a gun outside the gate. With obvious command, James convinced Qadhafi to withdraw, leaving the base in James's command until it was closed.

After leaving Libya, James was promoted to brigadier general at the Pentagon in 1970. Five years later, after he'd been named commander in chief of **NORAD (North American Air Defense Command)** he became the first African-American four star general.

ALEX HALEY
1921-1992

Alex Haley, perhaps the most successful man to employ television as a tool in teaching Americans about African-American history, turned his book *Roots* into a televised miniseries that attracted a rapt national audience.

Alex Haley was born in Ithica, New York, the first of three brothers. He grew up with not only a respectful love of storytelling, but a respectful sense of history through listening to his grandmother's stories while sitting on the porch in the evenings in Henning, Tennessee. There, she would remind the boys that their African and American history was longer than they or their parents could remember, and richer in experience than they themselves could imagine.

Alex graduated from high school at age 15, and joined the Coast Guard in 1939. He practiced writing constantly, following the formulas of other successful writers and writing on any subject. When he returned from the Coast Guard, he took up writing full-time, just as the 1960s **civil rights movement** was building like a storm.

From 1954 to 1956, he was a freelance writer for *Atlantic Monthly* and *Playboy*. One of his interviews for *Playboy* was with the controversial **Malcolm X** (see no. 87). Together, Haley and Malcolm produced *The Autobiography of Malcolm X* in 1965, which gained massive popularity. Working on the history of one man was what inspired Haley to begin his landmark work, *Roots*.

Roots, which took 12 years to research, is the story of Haley's ancestral history, from before his ancestor **Kunta Kinte** was captured in Africa and brought on a slave ship to America all the way through the generations to Haley himself. Published in 1977, *Roots* won a **Pulitzer Prize** and was made into a television miniseries that immortalized not just his own family's experience, but that of millions of African-Americans. By familiarizing 130 million viewers with the fascinating heritage of only one of the countless families who'd been brought to the US, Haley led Americans of all races to begin exploring their own family histories.

Having produced what, at the time, was the most watched program ever, Haley retired to complete only one other book before his death. The novella *A Different Kind of Christmas* was published in 1988, and his biography of **Madame C.J. Walker** (see no. 31) was never finished.

Alex Haley.

89

83. WHITNEY M. YOUNG, JR.
1920-1978

Whitney M. Young, Jr., who transformed the **National Urban League (NUL)** from an employment service into a major civil rights organization, was born in Lincoln Ridge, Kentucky. He studied at the all-black **Lincoln Model School** and its higher institution, the **Lincoln Institute**, which was headed by his father. He went to **Kentucky State College** and graduated with an M.A. in 1947, the same year he joined the St. Paul, Minnesota, branch of the National Urban League. By 1950, Young was the executive director of the National Urban League branch in Omaha, Nebraska.

Whitney M. Young. Jr.

The National Urban League was formed by the 1911 merger of three separate organizations—the **Committee for Improving the Industrial Conditions of Negroes in New York**, the **National League for the Protection of Colored Women** and the **Committee on Urban Conditions**. Formed to help integrate newly arrived African-Americans into the society of bigger cities, the National Urban League organized programs to introduce immigrants to employers. Focused on urban social concerns, the organization worked at finding jobs for people, training them, and mediating with white businesses willing to hire black employees.

In 1961, when Young was appointed executive director of the National Urban League, Dr. **Martin Luther King, Jr.** (see no. 91) was already active. The **civil rights movement** was just waiting for a catalyst — a woman like **Rosa Parks** (see no. 72), who was riding on a bus in Alabama and refused to give her seat to a white passenger.

When Rosa Parks' act of resistance set of the **Montgomery bus boycott** in 1955, th National Urban Leagu was forced to decid whether it would remai .an autonomous organ zation or become on that merged with th mass of Americans ri ing for civil liberty. was Young's leadersh that turned the Nation Urban League into on of the major supporte of the March on Was ington in 1963.

With Young in charge, the Nation Urban League went through a transitic that enlarged its scope of influence consi erably. Persuading the organization's lea ership to employ mass protest as a tool f social engineering, Young added its mer bers to the pool of national supporter "The Urban League will be valueless responsible institutions in our society if does not maintain communication with ar the respect of other responsible Negr organizations and the respect of the mass of Negro citizens."

Young remained executive director un his death in 1971, which occurred while I was attending the **African-American Di logue** in Nigeria. He is remembered as man who could build bridges, and as **Nan J. Weiss** said, "Young enlarged the econon ic opportunities available to black Amer cans....He gave powerful whites in the pr vate sector a means of comprehending tl problems of the ghetto and, in the most su cessful instances, made some contributic toward their amelioration...."

Leon Sullivan, founder of the **Opportunities Industrialization Centers of America (OIC)**, was born in Charleston, West Virginia. He became a Baptist minister while still in high school, and accepted an athletic scholarship to **West Virginia State College**. He then studied theology at **Union Theological Seminary** and **Columbia University** based on the recommendations of his mentor, Rev. **Adam Clayton Powell, Jr.** (see no. 68).

Leon Sullivan.

Sullivan learned the art of successful mass protest by watching Powell launch the "Don't buy where you can't work" campaign, encouraging African-Americans to spend their income in businesses that employed African-Americans. He also learned how to affect a crowd. Preaching at **First Baptist Church** of South Orange, New Jersey, and later at **Zion Baptist Church** in North Philadelphia, Sullivan spoke not just about God, but about money. With the goal of black economic independence, Sullivan organized boycotts that convinced Philadelphia businesses to hire over 3,000 more African-Americans by the year 1962.

Although the boycotts had a high rate of success, Sullivan realized he had only begun. Continuing to support only businesses that would hire African-Americans, Sullivan began to train the new employees, who were being placed in jobs for which they had not been sufficiently educated. His projects came to the attention of Dr. **Martin Luther King, Jr.** (see no. 91), who developed a new department for the **Southern Christian Leadership Conference** — Operation Breadbasket — which, under the leadership of Rev. **Jesse Jackson** (see no. 99), supported the hiring and training of African-Americans in all the nation's major cities.

Meanwhile, Sullivan was gathering funds from his congregation to form a new organization, the Opportunities Industrialization Centers of America (OIC), which employed African-Americans as trainers for others entering the workforce. The more Sullivan worked, the more he saw was needed. After finding jobs for African-Americans, training these new employees, affecting the strongest civil rights organizations in the nation, and employing a staff of his own, Sullivan saw it was necessary to take African-Americans further into the business of doing business: "We're going to have to develop literally thousands of entrepreneurs who know business for business' sake." Sullivan then began a venture capital company. His congregation invested in shopping plazas, garment factories, aerospace enterprises and apartment complexes — all owned by African-Americans.

Sullivan's own business sense led him to the board of directors at **General Motors** in 1971, and allowed him to develop "the **Sullivan Principles**," which shaped US policy against apartheid in South Africa. With the help of these principles, South African prisoners were freed, and American businesses that indirectly fed apartheid by feeding the South African economy pulled their support. The boycott, though it hurt South Africa's black consumers, led ultimately to the collapse of apartheid, making a multiracial democracy possible.

James Baldwin, one of America's finest writers, was born in Harlem during the electrifying **Harlem Renaissance** (see no. 36). Beginning to preach at age 14, following his father Rev. **David Baldwin**'s example, Baldwin was using his youth to pull an audience when he took over as editor of his high school newspaper. After spending much of his youth in libraries writing plays, short stories and poetry, he finally connected with other young people interested in reading and writing. He soon fell away from the church and devoted himself to writing.

Baldwin left home early and soon met novelist **Richard Wright** (see no. 69), who helped him secure a **Eugene Saxon Memorial Trust Award**. Baldwin had already begun his first novel, which was published in 1953 as *Go Tell It On the Mountain*, but put it aside to complete a short story, "Previous Condition," which was published in 1948.

Though his talent was evident at a young age, Baldwin lived with a sense of conflict that drove him from the US to Paris, where he found it easier to write honestly about the difficulties of being black in white intellectual circles. His first published essay, "Everybody's Protest Novel" was written in his first year in Paris, but it sharply criticized Richard Wright's *Native Son* and severed their friendship. Baldwin had a nervous breakdown due to the stress of losing his mentor, which was intensified by his financial difficulties. He recuperated in Switzerland, where he finally completed *Go Tell It on the Mountain.*

Baldwin soon returned to Europe to begin *Another Country* and the brilliant play *The Amen Corner.* He put them aside, and wrote what would become his own favorite novel, *Giovani's Room.* It was followed by the collection of essays *Nobody Knows My Name* (1960), *Another Country*, completed in 1962, his exquisite and famous work, *The Fire Next Time* (1963)

and *No Name in the Street* (1972). Altogether, Baldwin wrote 16 books, along with two plays produced on **Broadway,** *The Amen Corner* and *Blues for Mr. Charlie.*

Even while writing in the 1950s and 60s Baldwin was actively involved in the social upheaval of the civil rights movement. He worked closely with civil rights groups where his influential name could be helpful. Devoted to nonviolence and the maintenance of personal integrity even in the face of ugliness, Baldwin urged African-Americans to stand above their oppressors and maintain a sense of pride stronger than the insult of racism.

Baldwin continued to write until his death, finishing *The Evidence of Things Not Seen* in 1985. His funeral, held in the Cathedral of St. John the Divine, was attended by more than 4,000 mourners. Both **Maya Angelou** (see no. 89) and **Toni Morrison** (see no. 93) came to pay their respects, and spoke of Baldwin's place in history as one of America's greatest writers.

James Baldwin.

Shirley St. Hill Chisholm was the first African-American woman elected to the **US Congress** and the first African-American to launch a campaign for a major party presidential nomination. She was born in Brooklyn, where she stayed until the age of three. Sent to her maternal grandmother in Barbados, Chisholm lived away from her parents until they could afford her education. In 1934 she returned to New York, graduating cum laude from **Brooklyn College** in 1946. She attended **Columbia University** for graduate work in elementary education and worked as a teacher before joining the New York City Bureau of Child Welfare, and molding the **Unity Democratic Club** into an organized body for the support of district reforms.

Launching a political career in 1964, when she was elected the first African-American assemblywoman from Brooklyn, Chisholm proved herself a powerful supporter of women and African-Americans. She was reelected in 1965 and 1966, and launched her campaign for a congressional seat from the 12th district in 1968. Her election made her the first African-American woman in Congress, and her reputation as a maverick who crossed party lines made her an excellent politician dedicated to the goals of equality.

In 1972, Chisholm used her excellent record to buoy her campaign for the Democratic Party's candidacy for the US presidency. She was the first African-American to make a serious attempt at the presidency and her courage would inspire other African-American leaders like Rev. **Jesse Jackson**

Shirley St. Hill Chisholm.

(see no. 99) to go further toward the nation's most influential political position.

Though Chisholm lost the nomination to **George McGovern**, she retained her position in Congress, reelected to her seat six times before her retirement in 1982. In the same year, she began teaching at **Mount Holyoke College**. In 1984 she founded the **National Political Congress of Black Women**, dedicated, as Chisholm has always been, to the elimination of racism and sexism in America and in American politics.

The NPCBW sent a delegation of 100 American women to the Democratic Convention in 1988 to remind the nation's politicians that civil rights issues needed constant attention. Her respected career made her President **Bill Clinton's** choice for United States ambassador to Jamaica in 1993.

Malcolm X was eulogized by **Ossie Davis** (see no. 77) after his assassination as "our manhood, our living black manhood....And we shall know him for what he was and is — a prince, our own black, shining prince, who did not hesitate to die because he loved us so." During the two centuries between **Crispus Attucks** (see no. 1) and Malcolm X, a revolution had occurred in the African-American psyche. African-Americans were now able to adore and admire a black leader because he embodied revolution, self-respect, and the steadfast rejection of any sublimation.

Malcolm X was born **Malcolm Little** in Omaha, Nebraska, the son of Rev. **Earl Little**, a bold Baptist preacher who moved his family to Lansing, Michigan after receiving consistent threats from the **Ku Klux Klan**. In Lansing, Little's house was firebombed in response to the minister's radical notions of social justice. When Malcolm was six, his father was murdered for his egalitarian ideals. Malcolm quit school in the eighth grade and went to the streets for his education. Deeply involved in a world of drugs, crime and prostitution in Detroit and Harlem, New York, he was jailed in 1946 for burglary. His six year sentence taught his soul to thrive.

Malcolm joined the **Nation of Islam** in 1948. He studied the Honorable **Elijah Muhammad**'s teachings and spent his time reading encyclopedias, learning new words from the dictionary, and honing his intellect on the teachings of the **Black Muslims**. He met Elijah Muhammad in 1952, while on parole, and was later invited to join him in Chicago. Malcolm X, using the new name given him, rose to the second highest position in the sect. For nearly 12 years, Malcolm X's

Malcolm X.

pride, intelligence, and effec tive speeches drew new mem bers to the Nation of Islam Teaching African-American to embrace rather than hate th color of their skin, find pride i their heritage and their accom plishments, and rebel agains any form of racism, Malcolr X embodied the "black prince of Davis' speech.

In 1963, after Malcolm X success as an orator and a organizer had earned him h own following, Elijah Muhammad decide that Malcolm X's power was out of hand. H suspended Malcolm X for 90 days after hear ing him state that **John F. Kennedy**'s assass nation amounted to "chickens coming hom to roost." Malcolm X responded by formin the **Organization of Afro-American Unity** After a trip to **Mecca** in 1964, he converte to **Orthodox Islam**, returning to the US wit a new tolerance. He had walked among me of every color, all taking the pilgrimag required of every Muslim, and heard th words of **Muhammad**, "**The Prophet**." H changed his name to **El-Hajj Malik El Shabazz** and denounced Elijah Muhamma publicly.

Never afraid of the consequences of hi statements, Malcolm X ignored the deat threats that followed and kept his publi engagements, including the one at th **Audubon Ballroom** in Harlem on Februar 21, 1965. As he began to speak to the crowd he was shot to death. Three Black Muslim were convicted for murder, though th Nation of Islam denied any involvemen Malcolm X's death was one of the two mos painful blows to the progressing **civil right movement**. The second was the death of D **Martin Luther King, Jr.** (see no. 91), wh opposed Malcolm X's tactics, but supporte his ideal of complete equality.

HARRY BELAFONTE
b. 1927

Harry Belafonte, who pursued a career in movies and music while supporting the **civ- rights movement**, was born a first genera- on American in New York. At age eight, e returned to his mother's native Jamaica or five years, moving back to New York to tend high school in Harlem for two years efore joining the navy in 1944.

It was after his return to the US that Bela- onte fell in love with the theater. While oing janitorial work, someone gave him ckets to *Home Is the Hunter*, and Belafonte as impressed enough to join the Dramatic Vorkshop of the **New School for Social esearch** in New York. He was heard singing ne of his original songs during a production, nd was immediately signed to a jazz club alled the **Royal Roost**. He launched his pop- lar singing career, touring for two years efore deciding to quit. He then became namored with African inspired Caribbean olk music and its cousin, calypso.

A world class performer, Belafonte pro- moted these two styles, and popularized African-based rhythms. Throughout the 1950s and 1960s, he crossed all lines, gain- ing a reputation throughout America and the world, developing a name that he often lent to the support of civil rights crusaders led by Dr. **Martin Luther King, Jr.** (see no. 91). Holding a special place in the move- ment because he was such a celebrity, Bela- fonte was sought out by **John F. Kennedy** and became influential in forming an alliance between Kennedy and King. He organized a massive march for school inte- gration with **Bayard Rustin** (see no. 71), and was instrumental in securing celebrity support for the 1963 **March on Washington**. His name held a lot of weight both in the African-American community and the broader entertainment industry, and he was often able to enlist the popular public enter- tainers who swayed the opinions of so many Americans.

Even while he was assisting King and others, Belafonte was supporting a massive career as an entertainer. Appearing in *Bright Road* (1953), *Carmen Jones* (1954), *The World, the Flesh, and the Devil* (1959), *Odds Against Tomorrow* (1959), *Buck and the Preacher* (1972), and *Uptown Saturday Night* (1974), he maintained a high profile and a reputation as a dazzling screen star. But his main source of pride continued to be his involvement in the civil rights move- ment: "A couple of Broadway shows closed down at night to let some of the artists come, as they had done also at the March on Washington....I was very proud of us, many of us black and white who did that."

Belafonte continues to be active. In 1990, he organized a reception for South Africa's new president, **Nelson Mandella**, and celebrated the **Universal Declaration of the Human Rights of the Child** with the **United Nations**.

Harry Belafonte.

Maya Angelou, the **US Poet Laureate**, was born **Marguerite Johnson** in St. Louis, Missouri. She and her brother **Bailey** left their parents' home for their grandmother's house when Maya was only four. She graduated from the eighth grade in Stamps, Arkansas, and she and her brother moved to San Francisco to be reunited with their mother, who had left Missouri after divorcing their father. All of these years are detailed in the first of Maya Angelou's autobiographical books: *I Know Why the Caged Bird Sings* (1970). The honest and sensitive stories of a young girl's struggle to survive made Angelou one of contemporary America's most valued writers, yet it was only the first in a lifetime of achievements.

Maya, which is what her brother called her, studied drama and dance at the **California Labor School** while attending George Washington High. At the age of 16, she had an son, and faced all the moral judgements of a racist, sexist society. To describe the difficulties of being a single parent, Maya wrote *Gather Together in My Name* (1974). Intimate and vivid, it too increased her standing as a writer, as did her three other autobiographies, each detailing the development of an exceptional talent. *Singin' and Swingin' and Gettin' Merry Like Christmas* (1976) follows her through her theatrical career, which took her all over the world on tour with *Porgy and Bess*. *The Heart of Woman* (1981) is about her maturity as an artist, and *All God's Children Need Traveling Shoes* explains her time in Africa, where she edited an Egyptian publication and lectured in Ghana. It follows her back to America and details her involvement in the activist 1960s.

Her first screenplay, "*Georgia, Georgia*" (1972), became the first pro-duced screenplay written and directed by a African-American woman.

Maya Angelou went on to make histor as one of America's finest poets. Her pub lished collections, including *Give Me a Coo Drink of Water 'Fore I Die* (1971), *Oh Pra My Wings Are Gonna Fit Me Well* (1975 *Still I Rise* (1978), *Shaker, Why Don't Yo Sing* (1983), *Poems: Maya Angelou* (1986 *Now Sheba Sings the Song* (1987), and *Shall Not Be Moved* (1990) all preceded he brilliant reading at the inauguration of Pres ident **Bill Clinton** in 1992.

Named poet laureate for the natior Maya Angelou has become more than a artist with endurance, vitality and powe She has become a national symbol fc excellence.

Maya Angelou.

Lerone Bennett, Jr. is the author of *Before the Mayflower: A History of the Negro in America*, and other texts that highlight African-American history while weaving it into the story of American history. He was born in Clarksdale, Mississippi, and attended segregated schools in nearby Jackson, where he worked on his school newspaper, developing an early passion for succinct, readable prose. He edited the *Mississippi Enterprise* after graduation and went to **Morehouse College**, earning a B.A. in 1949. He started reporting for the *Atlanta Daily World* in the same year, graduating to city editor in 1952. He kept the position for a year before becoming associate editor for **John Johnson**'s *Jet* magazine (see no. 79).

Finding himself in the **Johnson Publishing Company**, one of the most influential black-owned businesses of the 1950s, Bennett saw the opportunity to direct the opinions of a huge readership. When he took over the position of senior editor for the nine-year-old *Ebony* magazine in 1958, he was able to write and publish his own articles on the subject that interested him most — the history of black America.

By 1962, Bennett had developed not only a broad body of work that could stand as a major collection, but a style that was both readable and exciting. He used both to create the influential text *Before the Mayflower*. Reprinted many times, this text stands as one of the finest cohesive histories in America. It was the first of many pieces that would earn Bennett a reputation among scholars and laymen alike. In 1964, *The Negro Mood and Other Essays* was published. *What Manner of Man?* (1964),

Lerone Bennett, Jr.

which tells the story of Dr. **Martin Luther King, Jr.** (see no. 91), *Confrontation, Black and White* (1965), *Black Power, USA, The Human Side of Reconstruction 1867-1877* (1967), *Pioneers in Protest* (1968), *The Challenge of Blackness* (1972), *The Shaping of Black America* (1974), and *Wade in the Water: Great Moments in Black History* (1979) are all evidence of the illuminating quality of his work.

Continuing to communicate the complex and compelling story of African-American evolution, Bennett added an up-to-date perspective to *Before the Mayflower*, and released a new edition in 1982, making it a contemporary favorite of researchers and students.

Rev. Dr. **Martin Luther King, Jr.**, the most influential man ever to fight for the rights of African-Americans, was born into a lineage of preachers who brought the family from slavery to a prominent social position in Atlanta, Georgia. Knowing that the church was a tool for justice and leadership, King began his career as a reverend immediately after college, and ended it as a hero.

Dr. Martin Luther King, Jr.

King led the **Montgomery bus boycott**, launched after **Rosa Parks** (see no. 72) refused to yield her bus seat to a white man in 1955. By preaching the "gospel of freedom" and organizing nonviolent protest in the tradition of **Mahatma Gandhi**, King maintained the boycott for 381 days, and the **US Supreme Court** declared bus segregation unconstitutional. It was the victory the **civil rights movement** had been waiting for, and King was its chosen leader.

For seven years, King led boycotts, sit-ins and marches designed to demolish segregationist policies. In 1957, King formed the **Southern Christian Leadership Conference (SCLC)**, which became one of the dominant organizations of the movement. In 1963, King ignored an order barring protests and marched through Birmingham with a small number of supporters. He was jailed by Police Commissioner **"Bull" Connor**, and during his confinement wrote the eloquent "Letter From Birmingham City Jail": "You speak of our activity in Birmingham as extreme....I wish you had commended the Negro sit-inners and demonstrators of Birmingham for their sublime courage, their willingness to suffer, and their amazing discipline....One day the South will recognize its real heroes...."

With the support of **A. Philip Randolph** (see no. 48), **Bayard Rustin** (see no. 71),

Roy Wilkins (see no. 62) President **John F. Kennedy** and the nation's most popular black celebrities, King' zenith came during a speech given to over 250,000 people who gathered in Washington to support civil rights.

King stood and defined the hope that had supported generations: "I have a dream that one day this nation will rise up and live out the true meaning of its creed: 'We hold these truths to be self-evident; that all men are created equal'....When we let freedom ring, when we let it ring from every village and hamlet, from every state and every city, we will be able to speed up the day when all of God's children...will be able to join hands and sing, in the words of the old Negro spiritual: 'Free at last! Free at last! Thank God Almighty, we are free at last.' "

King would live to see his effort rewarded by the **Civil Rights Act of 1964** which removed the poll taxes imposed by some Southern states, promised fair hiring practices and assured equal access to public amenities. He would celebrate the **1965 Voting Rights Act**, which destroyed all arbitrary barriers to voting, and he would accept the **Nobel Peace Prize** in 1967, but he would tragically miss the end of his final campaign: the sanitation workers' strike of 1968. As he stepped onto the balcony of the **Lorraine Motel** on April 4, an assassin's bullet ended his life, and ripped the heart from a movement at its zenith.

Rev. Dr. **Martin Luther King, Jr.'s** words, far from forgotten, have inspired worldwide support of human rights. His speeches and books are always available, and his biography, *Parting the Waters* by **Taylor Branch**, won the **Pulitzer Prize** in 1988.

LORRAINE HANSBERRY
1930-1965

Lorraine Hansberry, playwright and civ-rights activist, was born in Chicago, where her parents were always politically active. Unsatisfied with segregationist housing policies, they moved their family into an all-white neighborhood on the South Side when Lorraine was eight years old. Enduring threat, harassment and insult, the family stayed until a lower court ruling forced them out. Unbeaten, **Carl Hansberry** took the case to the **US Supreme Court**. In 1940, the segregationist policy was struck down. This was the defining event of Lorraine's youth, and it made for the subject of the first play on **Broadway** written by an African-American woman.

Once Lorraine had graduated from Englewood High School in 1948, she attended the **University of Wisconsin**, leaving after two years of theater to study painting at numerous schools, including the Art Institute of Chicago. She met **Paul Robeson** (see no. 57), who was publishing *Freedom*, and became the magazine's associate editor in 1952.

In 1957, after her marriage to **Robert Nemiroff**, Hansberry wrote the first draft of what would become one of the most informative and important plays to hit Broadway, *A Raisin in the Sun*. Named after a line from **Langston Hughes**' poem "Harlem" (see no. 64), *A Raisin in the Sun* told the story of the young black family she had grown up in as they tried to build a home for themselves in a white neighborhood.

Not only was the play written with an extremely sensitive hand, it struck a nerve among the white and black communities poised for the explosive struggle just ahead. Succeeding in New Haven, and then Philadelphia, Hansberry's first play opened on Broadway on March 11, 1959, creat-ing an overnight sensation. It ran for over a year and a half, won the **New York Drama Critics Circle Award** for **Best Play of the Year**, and featured artists who would change the face of the Broadway industry, including **Sidney Poitier, Ruby Dee** (see no. 77), and **Lou Gossett**.

Hansberry, an immediate celebrity, was asked to speak on civil rights and women's issues, and privately with **John F. Kennedy**. She went on to write the text for an influential photo documentary of the era called *The Movement: Documentary of a Struggle for Racial Equality in the US* (1964). Her other works include *The Sign in Sidney Brustein's Window* (1965), and after her untimely death in 1965 due to cancer, *To Be Young, Gifted, and Black: Lorraine Hansberry in Her Own Words*, adapted by her husband, and *Les Blancs: The Collected Last Plays of Lorraine Hansberry*, edited by Nemiroff and released in 1972.

Lorraine Hansberry.

Toni Morrison, born **Chloe Anthony Wofford** in Lorain, Ohio, grew up to be one of the most significant novelists of this age. Born during the **Depression**, she experienced the extreme poverty that African-Americans often faced. She was the daughter of sharecroppers who moved to Ohio after losing their land in Greenville, Alabama.

Morrison was an excellent student who completed her B.A. at **Howard University** in 1953 and her M.A. at **Cornell University** two years later. She began teaching at **Texas Southern University** in 1955, but left her post to teach at Howard University from 1957 to 1964. She wrote short stories, changed her name to Toni Morrison, and in 1964 began to edit textbooks for Random House. She was promoted to senior editor of the trade division, moved to New York City, and wrote her first novel, *The Bluest Eye*, in 1969. Based on the story of a black girl who yearns for a white concept of beauty, *The Bluest Eye* touched a new chord in American readers.

It was followed by *Sula* (1973), and *Song of Solomon*, which won the **National Book Critics Circle Award** in 1977. The following year, President **Jimmy Carter** appointed Morrison to the **National Council of the Arts**. *Tar Baby* (1981) was followed by *Beloved*, which won the 1987 **Pulitzer Prize for Literature**. *Jazz*, her most recent work, won the 1993 **Nobel Prize for Literature**.

While writing, and editing for Random House, Morrison still continued to teach. From **State University of New York** in 1969 to **Yale University** in 1975, to **Bard College** from 1979 to 1980, Morrison used her poetic intimate voice to explore "things that had never been articulated printed or imagined...about black girls, black women...."

In 1984, Morrison retired from publishing and became the humanities chair at the State University of New York at Albany. She left when **Princeton University** offered her the **Robert Goheen Professorship on the Council of the Humanities**, making her the first African-American woman writer to hold a named chair at an Ivy League university.

Along with her novels, which are held up among the nation's best, Morrison has recently written a play, *Dreaming Emmett*, and published a book of essays entitled *Playing in the Dark* (1992).

Toni Morrison.

BILL COSBY
b. 1937

Bill Cosby, whose highly accessible humor has endeared him to fans of all races, was born in Philadelphia, Pennsylvania. He attended Central High School for a year before transferring to Germantown High School, where he dropped out after his sophomore year in 1952. Cosby worked odd jobs for three years before joining the US Navy. He left the military and accepted an athletic scholarship to **Temple University** in 1960, where he played football and worked part time as a bartender. While warming up audiences at **The Underground**, Cosby discovered the appeal of his own comedic voice. He went to work at Greenwich Village's **Gaslight** in 1962 as a stand-up comedian and quit Temple to tour the nation.

Bill Cosby.

After his marriage to **Camille Hanks** in 1964, Cosby joined the cast of "I Spy," for which he was awarded television's highest acknowledgement, the **Emmy**. The show was cancelled in 1968, but Cosby was a successful star by then. He starred in the popular "Bill Cosby Show," as well as other projects that kept him in the public eye, before launching the phenomenally successful "Cosby Show" in 1984. This television sit-com proved how much had changed in the public definition of race. Based on the family of a successful doctor and the aches and pains of growing up together, "The Cosby Show" became the most popular show on television, and held that position for years before signing off in 1992.

Bill Cosby's family humor highlights how little difference there is between contemporary black and white Americans. With familiar concerns, familiar pleasures, familiar affections, Cosby has proved that African-Americans are first and foremost Americans.

Cosby continues to use his humor as a way of bridging societal gaps. Publishing three best-sellers, *Fatherhood* (1985), *Time Flies* (1987), and *Love and Marriage* (1989), Cosby is constantly finding the humor in all American life, even the most innocent events of the American family.

Although he's achieved immense success and popularity as an entertainer and philanthropist, sadly his private life revealed another side of his character. Numerous women came forward to tell their stories and accused Cosby of sexual assaults and related misconduct. Despite his denial of the allegations, in 2018 a jury found him guilty of three counts of aggravated indecent assault and was sentanced to three to ten years in state prison.

95. COLIN POWELL
b. 1937

Colin Powell, appointed by former president **George Bush** to chairman of the **Joint Chiefs of Staff**, was born in Harlem in New York City. He went to Morris High School in the South Bronx and **College of New York**, from which he graduated in 1958 with a B.S. in geology. He also joined the Reserve Officers Training Corps, where he became a second lieutenant upon graduation. He served in Vietnam and entered **George Washington University** after two tours of duty. He married **Vivian Johnson** in 1963

Graduating with an MBA in 1971, Powell was educated in more than just business. He had received a **White House Fellowship** the same year and had already been exposed to the daily politics of Washington. Though he continued to climb through the ranks in the military from 1972 to 1978, it was the **Jimmy Carter** administration

Colin Powell.

that brought him back into the complex world of White House politics. As executive assistant to the secretary of energy, and then as senior military assistant to the deputy secretary of defense successively from 1979 to 1986, Powell began a new ascent. He was sent to Frankfurt, Germany, where he was named commanding general of a US Army Corps before returning to assist **Frank Carlucci**, the president's national security advisor, and the **National Security Council (NSC)**.

When Carlucci was promoted to secretary of defense, Powell succeeded him as national security advisor. Through successive positions, Powell had learned how to affect national policies on security and trade. He was also a respected advisor on domestic issues like education and the environment.

Already a visible, key player in national and international affairs, it was President

George Bush who promoted Colin Powell to "the most powerful military position in the world," as writer **Columbus Salley** wrote. In 1989, Colin Powell was named chairman of the Joint Chiefs of Staff. It was the highest honor a military man could receive.

When Iraq invaded Kuwait in August 1990, it was Powell who was in control of organizing **Operation Desert Storm**, ultimately forcing Iraqi troops out of that oil-rich country in February, 1991.

Operation Desert Storm was clearly the most advanced, impressive, high-tech war ever waged, and its effects were nearly instantaneous. Less than a month of full warfare waged by the Allies against Iraq was all it took to end an internationally threatening situation.

Colin Powell was reappointed by President George Bush in 1991 and retired in 1993.

Marian Wright Edelman, dedicated civil rights activist and founder of the **Children's Defense Fund (CDF)**, was born in Bennettsville, South Carolina. She was the daughter of parents who advocated grassroots social programs, and founded the **Wright Home for the Aged**, which Marian's mother ran. Marian attended segregated schools, and excelled at **Spelman College**, where she was offered a stipend to study at the **Sorbonne** in Paris and the **University of Geneva** in Switzerland. She returned to Spelman in 1959 for her senior year, during which she participated in the sit-ins and protests that were integrating the South. She graduated valedictorian in 1960 and was so engaged with the **civil rights movement** that she dropped her plans to study international relations, and went to **Yale University Law School** instead.

She was active in a voter registration drive in Mississippi during 1963, interned with the Jackson, Mississippi NAACP, and headed the **NAACP Legal Defense and Educational Fund** between 1964 and 1968. In 1968, the **Field Foundation** awarded her a grant that allowed her to found the **Washington Research Project**, which began Wright's lifelong journey to understand the effects of poverty on children, and find the solutions to the problems faced primarily by African-Americans.

Wright's research was so powerful that she founded the CDF to affect political policy and secure the funds and the political support that could alleviate the pressures of poverty on America's children. She viewed CDF's mission as educating Americans about how to take preventative action in the areas of health, education, child care, youth employment, child welfare and family support services. In 1987, the CDF introduced the Act for Better Child Care, bringing children's health to the forefront of the discussion on how to strengthen America in a newly globalized economy.

Edelman has received over 35 awards for her work, including the **Albert Schweitzer Humanitarian Prize** (1988), and has produced a published body of work on the needs and concerns of the nation's quietest population. *Children Out of School in America* was published in 1974, *School Suspensions: Are They Helping Children* in 1975, *Portrait of Inequality: Black and White Children in America* in 1980, *Families in Peril: An Agenda for Social Change* in 1987 and *The Measure of Our Success* in 1992.

Marian Wright Edelman.

Wilma Rudolph, who overcame crippling polio to win three gold medals in track events at the 1960 **Summer Olympics**, was born in Bethlehem, Tennessee, 17th in a line of 19 children. Born prematurely, she had to fight for her life from the beginning. Wilma spent her early childhood bedridden, susceptible to everything, and surrounded by an enormous family. Though Wilma was always struggling to regain her health, the hardest fight was the one she waged against polio, which struck when she was four years old. Told she would never walk again, Wilma was confined to her bed, but her parents refused to accept defeat and waged a family war against the effects of the disease.

Every member of the family was put to the task of massaging and exercising Wilma's leg muscles, performing an early form of physical therapy. Wilma's mother took time off from her job as a maid to drive her daughter to a specialist 90 miles away once a week, and slowly, through constant effort, Wilma began to improve. By the time she was eight, she could walk again with the help of a brace. Soon after that, she was able to walk without the brace, though she had to wear a special shoe. Finally she could go to school. Her limp was pronounced at first, but Wilma accepted challenges like a winner. She began playing basketball with her many brothers, strengthening her muscles, her agility, and her balance, and practicing by herself once she'd worn them out. At age 11 Wilma performed what would have seemed like a miracle to the doctors who had doubted her. She took off her special shoe and played basketball barefoot, proving once and for all that she had mastered the use of her legs.

Basketball was the sport she had taught herself to excel in and she kept with it becoming an all-state high school champion when she was 15. She scored 803 points in the space of 25 games, breaking the state record for girls' basketball. At the same time, she was excelling in track and field.

As a senior in high school, Rudolph qualified for the 1956 Olympics, held in Melbourne, Australia. She won a bronze medal in the 400-meter relay and came home determined to go even further. She qualified again in 1960, and this time went to Rome, Italy where she not only won a gold medal in the 400-meter relay, but also in the 100- and 200-meter relays. Voted **US Female Athlete of the Year** by the **Associated Press**, Wilma Rudolph returned to the United States as "the fastest woman in the world."

Wilma Rudolph

Bill Gray, who was majority whip of the Democratic Party in Congress before becoming president and CEO of the United Negro College Fund (UNCF), was born in Baton Rouge, Louisiana. He followed the example of his father, Dr. William Herbert Gray II, who was president of Florida Normal and Industrial College (1941-44) and Florida A&M College (1944-49) and left to become the pastor of the Bright Hope Baptist Church in Philadelphia,.

Gray grew up with his father's passion for both religion and education. He graduated from Franklin & Marshall College in 1963 with a B.A, and from Drew Technology Seminary in 1966 with a Master of Divinity degree. He received a Master of Theology degree from Princeton in 1970, and succeeded his father and his grandfather as pastor at the Bright Hope Baptist Church after his father's death in 1972.

From his beginning at Bright Hope, Gray was a dedicated organizer, building non-profit housing corporations, and running for Congress for the first time in 1976. Though he lost to the incumbent, Robert Nix, he ran again in 1978, and was elected to the Second Congressional District for six consecutive terms, retiring by choice to preside over the UNCF in 1992.

Gray's presence in Congress was always influential. In 1985, when he was elected to chair the House Budget Committee, it was because his reputation had led him to distinction as a man capable of passing a budget of trillions of dollars through Congress. Not only did he affect the national budget, but he did so with a special care for programs related to education, minimizing poverty and assisting those in need.

Gray was also a member of the Subcommittee on Foreign Operations, where he was able to author the Anti-Apartheid Acts of 1985 and 1986, both of which demanded that apartheid be abolished in South Africa

Bill Gray.

if US relations were to remain friendly. In 1992, when apartheid was abolished in South Africa and the presidency was won by Nelson Mandella, Gray was one of the men who could take credit for aiding the transition.

In 1989, Gray was elected to the third most powerful position in the Democratic Congress — majority whip. Though he would have been able to affect national policy indefinitely, Gray decided to retire from Congress in 1991 to become the CEO of the United Negro College Fund, causing a considerable shock in Washington and the rest of the nation.

What led Gray to his new career was his unfailing belief in education. Facing a world which he calls "a culture out of control," he took the most meaningful position possible in the struggle toward educational, economic and civil equality. Realizing that African-Americans face difficult challenges in present day America, he put the strength of his name and his reputation behind the thing he had undying faith in — education.

99. JESSE JACKSON
b. 1941

Rev. **Jesse Louis Jackson**, founder of the **Rainbow Coalition** and two-time candidate for the **Democratic Party**'s presidential nomination, was born in Greenville, South Carolina, where he excelled in high school football, baseball and basketball. He graduated in 1959 and accepted a football scholarship to the University of Illinois. Citing racism as the reason, Jackson left Illinois for the predominantly black **North Carolina A&T College**.

Rev. Jesse Jackson.

While at A&T, Jackson earned a reputation for being more than just an athlete. As student body president, he was a fearless public demonstrator, leading sit-ins that sometimes ended in massive arrests, while proclaiming "I'll go to jail and I'll go to the chain gang if necessary." He graduated in 1964 and attended **Chicago Theological Seminary** at the **University of Chicago** in 1965, following in the footsteps of some of the finest African-American leaders.

In 1965, Jackson met Dr. **Martin Luther King, Jr.** (see no. 91), who became his mentor until King's death in 1968. King named Jackson head of **Operation Breadbasket**, a highly influential program within the **Southern Christian Leadership Conference (SCLC)** designed to increase the economic power of African-Americans by involving them in white businesses that catered to black consumers. Extremely charismatic as an organizer and as a leader of boycotts, Jackson was able to expand the Chicago-based program until Operation Breadbasket was busy finding jobs for African-Americans in every major city of the nation.

Jackson left Operation Breadbasket in 1971 and founded **PUSH (People United to Save Humanity)**, which dedicated itself to increasing the economic power of African-

Americans. The spin-of program that Jackso launched in 1976, **PUSH fo Excellence**, was designe on the principle that educa tion was the greatest tool t success. Increasing the qual ity of African-America education was directly tie to increasing their power i American society whil improving the quality c life.

Jackson expanded hi interest to international issues, meetin with leaders in the Middle East in hopes c effecting peace. His main successes came i 1984, when he used his friendship with Sy ian leader **Hafez al-Assad** to free Navy pilc **Robert Goodman**, and his popularity i Cuba to free 48 American and Cuban pri oners.

In the same year, Rev. Jesse Jackson ra for the first time for the Democratic party' presidential nomination. Though h launched a highly visible campaign with th support of his "**Rainbow Coalition**," whic focused on the needs of Americans of all col ors and gained support, he lost to **Walte Mondale**. Running again in 1988, he lost **t Michael Dukakis**. Summing up the differ ence in the two campaigns, Jackson sai "...There were victories all over the place and there are still victories to be had, afte all. Mondale got 6.7 million votes and wor I got seven million and lost; Dukakis gc nine million." Because more Democra voted in 1988, the seven million votes which would have beat Mondale in 1984 weren't enough to beat Dukakis in 1988.

Jackson has continued his influenc upon American society with a highly suc cessful syndicated TV show, a position as shadow senator from Washington, D.C and numerous public appearances.

MUHAMMAD ALI
1942-2016

Muhammad Ali, who was called arguably the greatest fighter of all time" by Thomas Hauser, was born in Louisville, Kentucky, where he took up boxing at age 12. His bicycle had been stolen, and Ali, named Cassius Marcellus Clay, Jr. at birth, was learning to fight in order to beat up the kid who stole it. As Columbus Salley wrote, "By the time he finished high school, Ali had fought 108 times as an amateur boxer, won six Kentucky Golden Gloves championships, two National Golden Glove tournaments, and two national Amateur Athletic Union titles." Already considered the best in the world, Ali made it official in 1960, the year he took the Gold Medal at the Olympic Games in Rome, Italy.

Returning to the US to turn professional, Ali stole some of Gorgeous George's rhetoric, and picked up the talk that made him famous. Constantly proclaiming "I'm pretty, I'm the best....Float like a butterfly, sting like a bee...."

Ali gained national popularity, and an international reputation in 1964, when he beat the heavyweight champion Sonny Liston, becoming the new champion of the world. The day after he won the title, Ali publicly announced that he had joined the Nation of Islam (see no. 87), and accepted the new name bestowed on him by the Honorable Elijah Muhammad. From then on, he was Muhammad Ali, and no one ever forgot it.

Taking a firm stand in his open acceptance of the Black Muslim faith, Ali was prepared for the resistance that might come from his fans, but it was difficult to accept the US Army's response. Drafted in 1967, Ali refused to fight in the Vietnam War because of his religion. Not only was his refusal made public, but so was his bold argument against the war: "My enemy is the white people, not Viet Cong or Chinese or Japanese. You're my foes when I want free-dom. You're my foes when I want justice...." Convicted of draft evasion, Ali was stripped of his title and his boxing license was revoked. In 1971, the US Supreme Court reversed the decision, granting him conscientious objector status. His vindication added a new fire to his quest to regain his title. Fighting and beating George Foreman in 1984, Ali remained a nationally beloved champion until Leon Spinks took the title in February of 1978. In September of the same year, Ali fought Spinks again, won the title back and remained undefeated until his retirement in 1981.

When he left the world of boxing, he said, "Now my life is really starting. Fighting injustice, fighting racism, fighting crime, fighting illiteracy, fighting poverty, using this face the world knows so well, and going out and fighting for truth and different causes."

Muhammad Ali.

TRIVIA QUESTIONS & PROJECT SUGGESTIONS

1. Two African-Americans have tried to capture the Democratic candidacy for the US presidency. Who were they? (See nos. 86 and 99)

2. The Harlem Renaissance was an art movement that developed after World War II in New York City. Who were some of the many authors involved? (See nos. 32, 36, 37, 47, 52, 61, and 64)

3. The 1963 March on Washington brought over 250,000 Americans to Washington, DC in support of civil rights. What were the two pieces of civil rights legislation that passed within the next two years? (See nos. 62, 68, and 91)

4. There were two important movements that sprang up near the end of the 19th century. One turned into the National Association for the Advancement of Colored People. The other was based around a famous learning institution. What were the names of these two movements? How did they differ? In what ways were they the same? (See nos. 24 and 32)

5. Why did the Underground Railroad help slaves move safely to the North? (See no. 15)

6. Many musical forms emerged based on old spirituals brought from Africa. Name a couple of the forms that became popular and the musicians who popularized them. (See nos. 34, 54, 60, 75, and 88)

7. Matthew Henson, Dr. Charles Drew and Dr. Daniel Hale Williams were all responsible for being the first in the world to discover something. What did each of them do? (See nos. 25, 36 and 66)

8. What was "the Red Record?" (See no. 27)

9. Which husband and wife team met for the first time in the theater and went on to serve the civil rights movement? In what ways did they help improve the lives of African-Americans? (See no. 77)

10. What was the doctrine of *Plessy v Fergusson*? How did the *Brown v the Board of Education* Supreme Court case overturn it? (See nos. 55, 56, 67, and 74)

11. Madame C.J. Walker was the first female African-American millionaire. How did she do it? (See no. 31)

12. One athlete won four gold medals for his performance in the Olympic Games. Another overcame polio and won three gold medals. Who were they and in what years did they compete? (See nos. 73 and 97)

13. Malcolm X and Dr. Martin Luther King, Jr. were both great orators who believed in civil rights, but they differed in their beliefs about how to achieve them. What were the differences? (See nos. 87 and 91)

4. How did Alex Haley affect 130 million television viewers? Who were his two other books about? (See no. 82)

5. Many of the people included were journalists. Name three people who started their own publications. What were the names of their publications, and what were they about? (See nos. 8, 12, 14, 21, 32, 35, 38, 48, 61, and 79)

6. Who was the most important African-American film maker of the early 20th century? How did he differ from other film makers of the period? (See no. 45)

7. How did First Lady Eleanor Roosevelt help Marian Anderson break through racial boundaries? (See no. 63)

18. Colin Powell made world history in this decade. How did he do it? (See no. 95)

19. What event led to the founding of the first national African-American church? (See no. 6)

20. What was the black Back-to-Africa movement? (See nos. 12, 23 and 46)

21. In all fields, including politics, education, entertainment, religion, science, the arts, and medicine, there are men and women who have become our modern day heroes. Name one person from each field who inspires you.

INDEX

112